D0191303

# Death and Bereavement

Series Editor: Cara Acred

Volume 267

Independence Educational Publishers

First published by Independence Educational Publishers

The Studio, High Green

Great Shelford

Cambridge CB22 5EG

England

© Independence 2014

## Copyright

## Photocopy licence

## British Library Cataloguing in Publication Data

Death and bereavement. -- (Issues ; 267)

1. Bereavement.

I. Series II. Acred, Cara editor.

155.9'37-dc23

ISBN-13: 9781861686862

## Printed in Great Britain

MWL Print Group Ltd

# Contents

## Chapter 1: Grief and mourning

## Chapter 2: Death and end of life

# Introduction

**Death and Bereavement** is Volume 267 in the **ISSUES** series. The aim of the series is to offer current, diverse information about important issues in our world, from a UK perspective.

## ABOUT DEATH AND BEREAVEMENT

Death and bereavement are difficult topics to discuss, no matter what age you are. Nevertheless, they are an unavoidable part of life. This book explores how we cope with grief and loss, as well as some of the more perfunctory aspects of death such as organising a funeral and what happens to your digital data after you die.

## OUR SOURCES

Titles in the **ISSUES** series are designed to function as educational resource books, providing a balanced overview of a specific subject.

The information in our books is comprised of facts, articles and opinions from many different sources, including:

⇨ Newspaper reports and opinion pieces

⇨ Website factsheets

⇨ Magazine and journal articles

⇨ Statistics and surveys

⇨ Government reports

⇨ Literature from special interest groups.

## A NOTE ON CRITICAL EVALUATION

Because the information reprinted here is from a number of different sources, readers should bear in mind the origin of the text and whether the source is likely to have a particular bias when presenting information (or when conducting their research). It is hoped that, as you read about the many aspects of the issues explored in this book, you will critically evaluate the information presented.

It is important that you decide whether you are being presented with facts or opinions. Does the writer give a biased or unbiased report? If an opinion is being expressed, do you agree with the writer? Is there potential bias to the 'facts' or statistics behind an article?

## ASSIGNMENTS

In the back of this book, you will find a selection of assignments designed to help you engage with the articles you have been reading and to explore your own opinions. Some tasks will take longer than others and there is a mixture of design, writing and research-based activities that you can complete alone or in a group.

## FURTHER RESEARCH

At the end of each article we have listed its source and a website that you can visit if you would like to conduct your own research. Please remember to critically evaluate any sources that you consult and consider whether the information you are viewing is accurate and unbiased.

# Useful weblinks

www.childbereavement.org.uk

www.theconversation.com

www.deathcafe.com

www.dyingmatters.org

www.ehospice.com

www.funeralmap.co.uk

www.goodfuneralguide.co.uk

www.helpguide.org

www.kristiewest.com

www.mysendoff.com

www.ons.gov.uk

www.pet-loss.net

www.uk-sands.org

www.yougov.co.uk

www.winstonswish.org.uk

# Chapter 1

# Grief and mourning

# Coping with grief and loss

*Understanding the grieving process.*

*By Melinda Smith, M.A. and Jeanne Segal, Ph.D.*

Losing someone or something you love or care deeply about is very painful. You may experience all kinds of difficult emotions and it may feel like the pain and sadness you're experiencing will never let up. These are normal reactions to a significant loss. But while there is no right or wrong way to grieve, there are healthy ways to cope with the pain that, in time, can renew you and permit you to move on.

## What is grief?

Grief is a natural response to loss. It's the emotional suffering you feel when something or someone you love is taken away. The more significant the loss, the more intense the grief will be. You may associate grief with the death of a loved one – which is often the cause of the most intense type of grief – but any loss can cause grief, including:

⇨ Divorce or relationship break-up

⇨ Loss of health

⇨ Losing a job

⇨ Loss of financial stability

⇨ A miscarriage

⇨ Retirement

⇨ Death of a pet

⇨ Loss of a cherished dream

⇨ A loved one's serious illness

⇨ Loss of a friendship

⇨ Loss of safety after a trauma

⇨ Selling the family home.

The more significant the loss, the more intense the grief. However, even subtle losses can lead to grief. For example, you might experience grief after moving away from home, graduating from college, changing jobs, selling your family home, or retiring from a career you loved.

### Everyone grieves differently

Grieving is a personal and highly individual experience. How you grieve depends on many factors, including your personality and coping style, your life experience, your faith, and the nature of the loss. The grieving process takes time. Healing happens gradually; it can't be forced or hurried – and there is no 'normal' timetable for grieving. Some people start to feel better in weeks or months. For others, the grieving process is measured in years. Whatever your grief experience, it's important to be patient with yourself and allow the process to naturally unfold.

### Myths and facts about grief

MYTH: The pain will go away faster if you ignore it.

Fact: Trying to ignore your pain or keep it from surfacing will only make it worse in the long run. For real healing it is necessary to face your grief and actively deal with it.

MYTH: It's important to be 'be strong' in the face of loss.

Fact: Feeling sad, frightened, or lonely is a normal reaction to loss. Crying doesn't mean you are weak. You don't need to 'protect' your family or friends by putting on a brave front. Showing your true feelings can help them and you.

MYTH: If you don't cry, it means you aren't sorry about the loss.

Fact: Crying is a normal response to sadness, but it's not the only one. Those who don't cry may feel the pain just as deeply as others. They may simply have other ways of showing it.

MYTH: Grief should last about a year.

Fact: There is no right or wrong time frame for grieving. How long it takes can differ from person to person.

*Source: Center for Grief and Healing*

## Are there stages of grief?

In 1969, psychiatrist Elisabeth Kübler-Ross introduced what became known as the 'five stages of grief'. These stages of grief were based on her studies of the feelings of patients facing terminal illness, but many people have generalised them to other types of negative life changes and losses, such as the death of a loved one or a break-up.

### The five stages of grief:

⇨ Denial: 'This can't be happening to me.'

⇨ Anger: 'Why is this happening? Who is to blame?'

⇨ Bargaining: 'Make this not happen, and in return I will ____.'

⇨ Depression: 'I'm too sad to do anything.'

⇨ Acceptance: 'I'm at peace with what happened.'

If you are experiencing any of these emotions following a loss, it may help to know that your reaction is natural and that you'll heal in time. However, not everyone who grieves goes through all of these stages – and that's OK. Contrary to popular belief, you do not have to go through each stage in order to heal. In fact, some people resolve their grief without going through any of these stages. And if you do go through these stages of grief, you probably won't experience them in a neat, sequential order, so don't worry about what you 'should' be feeling or which stage you're supposed to be in.

Kübler-Ross herself never intended for these stages to be a rigid framework that applies to everyone who mourns. In her last book before her death in 2004, she said of the five stages of grief: 'They were never meant to help tuck messy emotions into neat packages. They are responses to loss that many people have, but there is not a typical response to loss, as there is no typical loss. Our grieving is as individual as our lives.'

### *Grief can be a roller coaster*

Instead of a series of stages, we might also think of the grieving process as a roller coaster, full of ups and downs, highs and lows. Like many roller coasters, the ride tends to be rougher in the beginning, the lows may be deeper and longer. The difficult periods should become less intense and shorter as time goes by, but it takes time to work through a loss. Even years after a loss, especially at special events such as a family wedding or the birth of a child, we may still experience a strong sense of grief.

*Source: Hospice Foundation of America*

## Common symptoms of grief

While loss affects people in different ways, many experience the following symptoms when they're grieving. Just remember that almost anything that you experience in the early stages of grief is normal –

including feeling like you're going crazy, feeling like you're in a bad dream, or questioning your religious beliefs.

⇨ Shock and disbelief – Right after a loss, it can be hard to accept what happened. You may feel numb, have trouble believing that the loss really happened, or even deny the truth. If someone you love has died, you may keep expecting him or her to show up, even though you know he or she is gone.

⇨ Sadness – Profound sadness is probably the most universally experienced symptom of grief. You may have feelings of emptiness, despair, yearning, or deep loneliness. You may also cry a lot or feel emotionally unstable.

⇨ Guilt – You may regret or feel guilty about things you did or didn't say or do. You may also feel guilty about certain feelings (e.g. feeling relieved when the person died after a long, difficult illness). After a death, you may even feel guilty for not

doing something to prevent the death, even if there was nothing more you could have done.

⇨ Anger – Even if the loss was nobody's fault, you may feel angry and resentful. If you lost a loved one, you may be angry with yourself, God, the doctors, or even the person who died for abandoning you. You may feel the need to blame someone for the injustice that was done to you.

⇨ Fear – A significant loss can trigger a host of worries and fears. You may feel anxious, helpless or insecure. You may even have panic attacks. The death of a loved one can trigger fears about your own mortality, of facing life without that person, or the responsibilities you now face alone.

⇨ Physical symptoms – We often think of grief as a strictly emotional process, but grief often involves physical problems, including fatigue, nausea, lowered immunity, weight loss or weight gain, aches and pains, and insomnia.

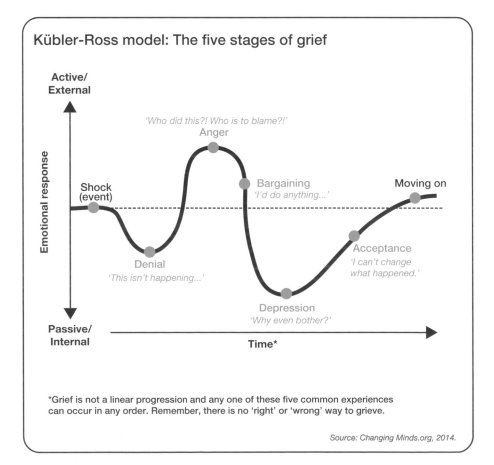

Kübler-Ross model: The five stages of grief

*Grief is not a linear progression and any one of these five common experiences can occur in any order. Remember, there is no 'right' or 'wrong' way to grieve.

*Source: Changing Minds.org, 2014.*

# Coping with grief and loss tip 1: Get support

The single most important factor in healing from loss is having the support of other people. Even if you aren't comfortable talking about your feelings under normal circumstances, it's important to express them when you're grieving. Sharing your loss makes the burden of grief easier to carry. Wherever the support comes from, accept it and do not grieve alone. Connecting to others will help you heal.

## Finding support after a loss

⇨ Turn to friends and family members - Now is the time to lean on the people who care about you, even if you take pride in being strong and self-sufficient. Draw loved ones close, rather than avoiding them, and accept the assistance that's offered. Oftentimes, people want to help but don't know how, so tell them what you need – whether it's a shoulder to cry on or help with funeral arrangements.

⇨ Draw comfort from your faith – If you follow a religious tradition, embrace the comfort its mourning rituals can provide. Spiritual activities that are meaningful to you – such as praying, meditating, or going to church – can offer solace. If you're questioning your faith in the wake of the loss, talk to a clergy member or others in your religious community.

⇨ Join a support group – Grief can feel very lonely, even when you have loved ones around. Sharing your sorrow with others who have experienced similar losses can help. To find a bereavement support group in your area, contact local hospitals, hospices, funeral homes, and counselling centres.

⇨ Talk to a therapist or grief counsellor – If your grief feels like too much to bear, call a mental health professional with experience in grief counselling. An experienced therapist can help you work through intense emotions and overcome obstacles to your grieving.

# Coping with grief and loss tip 2: Take care of yourself

When you're grieving, it's more important than ever to take care of yourself. The stress of a major loss can quickly deplete your energy and emotional reserves. Looking after your physical and emotional needs will help you get through this difficult time.

⇨ Face your feelings. You can try to suppress your grief, but you can't avoid it forever. In order to heal, you have to acknowledge the pain. Trying to avoid feelings of sadness and loss only prolongs the grieving process. Unresolved grief can also lead to complications such as depression, anxiety, substance abuse, and health problems.

⇨ Express your feelings in a tangible or creative way. Write about your loss in a journal. If you've lost a loved one, write a letter saying the things you never got to say; make a scrapbook or photo album celebrating the person's life; or get involved in a cause or organisation that was important to him or her.

⇨ Look after your physical health. The mind and body are connected. When you feel good physically, you'll also feel better emotionally. Combat stress and fatigue by getting enough sleep, eating right and exercising. Don't use alcohol or drugs to numb the pain of grief or lift your mood artificially.

⇨ Don't let anyone tell you how to feel, and don't tell yourself how to feel either. Your grief is your own, and no one else can tell you when it's time to 'move on' or 'get over it'. Let yourself feel whatever you feel without embarrassment or judgement. It's OK to be angry, to yell at the heavens, to cry or not to cry. It's also OK to laugh, to find moments of joy, and to let go when you're ready.

⇨ Plan ahead for grief 'triggers'. Anniversaries, holidays and milestones can reawaken memories and feelings. Be prepared for an emotional wallop, and know that it's completely normal. If you're sharing a holiday or life-cycle event with other relatives, talk to them ahead of time about their expectations and agree on strategies to honour the person you loved.

# When grief doesn't go away

It's normal to feel sad, numb, or angry following a loss. But as time passes, these emotions should become less intense as you accept the loss and start to move forward. If you aren't feeling better over time, or your grief is getting worse, it may be a sign that your grief has developed into a more serious problem, such as complicated grief or major depression.

## Complicated grief

The sadness of losing someone you love never goes away completely, but it shouldn't remain centre stage. If the pain of the loss is so constant and severe that it keeps you from resuming your life, you may be suffering from a condition known as complicated grief. Complicated grief is like being stuck in an intense state of mourning. You may have trouble accepting the death long after it has occurred or be so preoccupied with the person who died that it disrupts your daily routine and undermines your other relationships.

Symptoms of complicated grief include:

⇨ Intense longing and yearning for the deceased

⇨ Intrusive thoughts or images of your loved one

⇨ Denial of the death or sense of disbelief

⇨ Imagining that your loved one is alive

- ⇨ Searching for the person in familiar places
- ⇨ Avoiding things that remind you of your loved one
- ⇨ Extreme anger or bitterness over the loss
- ⇨ Feeling that life is empty or meaningless.

### The difference between grief and depression

Distinguishing between grief and clinical depression isn't always easy as they share many symptoms, but there are ways to tell the difference. Remember, grief can be a roller coaster. It involves a wide variety of emotions and a mix of good and bad days. Even when you're in the middle of the grieving process, you will have moments of pleasure or happiness. With depression, on the other hand, the feelings of emptiness and despair are constant.

Other symptoms that suggest depression, not just grief:

- ⇨ Intense, pervasive sense of guilt
- ⇨ Thoughts of suicide or a preoccupation with dying

- ⇨ Feelings of hopelessness or worthlessness
- ⇨ Slow speech and body movements
- ⇨ Inability to function at work, home, and/or school
- ⇨ Seeing or hearing things that aren't there.

Can antidepressants help grief?

As a general rule, normal grief does not warrant the use of antidepressants. While medication may relieve some of the symptoms of grief, it cannot treat the cause, which is the loss itself. Furthermore, by numbing the pain that must be worked through eventually, antidepressants delay the mourning process.

## When to seek professional help for grief

If you recognise any of the above symptoms of complicated grief or clinical depression, talk to a mental health professional right away. Left untreated, complicated grief and depression can lead to significant

emotional damage, life-threatening health problems, and even suicide. But treatment can help you get better.

Contact a grief counsellor or professional therapist if you:

- ⇨ Feel like life isn't worth living
- ⇨ Wish you had died with your loved one
- ⇨ Blame yourself for the loss or for failing to prevent it
- ⇨ Feel numb and disconnected from others for more than a few weeks
- ⇨ Are having difficulty trusting others since your loss
- ⇨ Are unable to perform your normal daily activities.

*February 2014*

- ⇨ The above information is reprinted with kind permission from Helpguide.org. Please visit www.helpguide.org for further information.

© Helpguide.org 2014

---

# Does the British 'stiff upper lip' still exist?

**What do you think about the famous 'British reserve'? Do you think the 'stiff upper lip' still exists, or has it disappeared in recent times?**

**By Jessica Henry**

Some people think of Britain as the nation of the 'stiff upper lip', meaning we are reserved, unemotional, or find it hard to show our feelings, especially in public. Social commentators often point to the death of Princess Diana as the turning point for the British reserve, suggesting that the outpouring of public grief indicated a new-found ability to display our emotions.

However, according to historian Dr Thomas Dixon, currently researching a project into the history of crying, the British actually have a long history of very public outpourings of grief – and our reputation for being emotionally

reserved is actually a fairly new thing.

What do you think about this 'stiff upper lip'? Was it ever a trait of the British, or has it evolved over the years? Is 'reservedness' something we, as Brits, are guilty of?

The majority of you thought that British people used to be more reserved, but have changed in recent years – although opinion was divided as to whether this was seen as a positive change or not!

Other participants argued that, comparatively speaking, the stiff upper lip mentality remains, especially when looking at

European or American culture, while some of you argued that the whole idea of 'British reserve' is a myth, unrepresentative of the population as a whole.

Here's what our poll participants had to say...

## What do you think about the 'stiff upper lip'?

**Argument 1: People in Britain used to be reserved, but no longer**

'Many forms of media and education over the past half century have eroded the myth that showing feelings is somehow a negative thing or even a sign of weakness. People today are encouraged to show their feelings.' Anon

'Over the last 20 years we have learnt how to communicate and technology encourages us to do so.' Anon

'We have taken on some traits of other cultures, especially American.' Tez, Merseyside

'Changes in schooling and discipline have made people less formal.' Anon

'The older generation are quite reserved and distant but the younger generation are more open and emotional.' Anon

'There is a constant stream of over-the-top emotional outpourings at all sorts of events from national tragedies to reality TV shows. The idea of the 'reserved' British is a myth now.' Anon

'In schools I think there is more emphasis on self-esteem and expressing yourself than there used to be.' Anon

'People are encouraged to air private problems, issues in public, including on TV and in magazines.' Lesley, London

### Argument 2: People in Britain today find it hard to show their feelings

'Compared to Americans or Europeans, the Brits find it hard to complain in case it causes offence.' Anon

'In our Americanised media, showing feelings and emotions is commonplace and encouraged; but in real life, this seems to be looked down upon – like it's a sign of weakness.' Anon

'Accounts from Europeans show that we are still relatively reserved.' Anon

'In the US I have been pleasantly surprised at how personable relationships can be with clients, peers and colleagues. I always felt I had to hide who I was as a person in professional settings in the UK.' Anon

'I travel a lot in my job and I find most people very reserved. They do not like to strike up conversations with 'strangers'; they only offer the minimum of help to get you out of their hair and rarely smile.' Anon

'The only emotion they do feel all comes out after a glass of wine after a hard day at the office.' Michelle, UK

'Although things are shifting, the majority of British citizens still tend to 'suffer in silence'. I believe this is a hangover from (or continuation of!) our country's feudal and class system.' Anon

### Argument 3: People in Britain

'I think that's a misconception brought about by the small number of aristocrats; real British people have always shown emotion.' Anon

'Living up north, people are a lot more friendly and open than those down south.' Mel H

'I believe this is an old wives' tale about the British, perhaps because other nations like the Americans can be so brash it makes us seem reserved in comparison which is no bad thing.' Ann

'The term "stiff upper lip" could only ever be applied to the upper class which is clearly not representative of the masses.' Colin K, Highlands

'There were a small group (mostly English middle and some upper class), for a short time who were encouraged to behave in this way – as well as a great many who were traumatised as a result of the effects of war.' Anon

'The "stiff upper lip" was a Victorian caricature. Jolly funny too.' Anon

'We're wonderfully eccentric in individual ways. Britain has never been reserved.' Joseph W, Leicester

### British vs American

Many of our participants noted a distinction between British and American behaviour.

Some felt that the British seem reserved in comparison to Americans, who they felt can appear more externally confident and outspoken. However, others argued that the Brits are by no means shy, retiring beasts – we have our eccentricities and colourful quirks.

What do you think about this distinction? Are Americans generally less reserved, or are they perhaps more reserved about certain issues? Why do you think this might be the case? And which kind of behaviour do you prefer?

*17 April 2012*

⇨ The above information is reprinted with kind permission from YouGov. Please visit www.yougov.co.uk for further information.

# Why prolonged grief should be listed as a mental disorder

**THE CONVERSATION**

*It's normal to have recurring waves of grief after the loss of a loved one but prolonged, severe grief requires treatment.*

*An article from The Conversation.*

*By Richard Bryant, Professor and Director of the Traumatic Stress Clinic at UNSW Australia*

Grief is one of the most universal and distressing experiences that humans suffer.

For most people, the emotional pain of losing someone close to them lasts for a relatively brief period. Many studies indicate that by six months after bereavement, most people begin to experience remission of the severe grief response. Waves of grief may come and go for months or years afterwards but these reactions don't impair or limit a person's capacity to engage in life's activities.

In contrast, a proportion of bereaved people (approximately 10% to 15%) suffer persistent grief that can last for many years. Many studies from different countries and cultural settings have documented that severe yearning for the deceased that persists beyond six months is associated with marked impairment and difficulty in engaging with people and in activities.

This is why the *Diagnostic and Statistical Manual of Mental Disorders, Fifth Edition (DSM-5)* has proposed a new diagnosis to represent this condition, known as adjustment disorder related to bereavement. The persistent yearning can be associated with difficulty accepting the death, feelings of loss of a part of oneself, anger about the loss, guilt or blame over the death, or difficulty in engaging with new social or other activities due to the loss. To meet diagnostic criteria, the symptoms must persist beyond six months after the death and affect the person's ability to function in day-to-day life.

The World Health Organization's proposed *International Classification of Diseases 11th Revision (ICD-11)* also includes a new diagnosis, termed prolonged grief disorder, which is defined similarly.

There has been enormous and emotive debate over the extent to which prolonged grief should be recognised as a mental disorder.

Traditionally, the *DSM* has precluded grief as a diagnostic disorder on the basis that it is 'an expectable and culturally sanctioned response to a particular event'. Supporting this line, opponents of the new diagnosis argue that grief is:

⇨ a ubiquitous condition insofar as death and loss is part of being human, and so emotional pain that is felt following bereavement should not be medicalised

⇨ managed differently across cultures and so a single diagnostic system cannot apply to all cultures

⇨ unlike most other psychological responses in that it is closely interwoven into religious practices

⇨ adequately described by existing anxiety and depression reactions so there's no need to identify it as a distinct construct.

Supporting the introduction of the new diagnosis is compelling data that counters these criticisms. First, factor analytic studies demonstrate that the key feature of the grief response (yearning for the deceased) is distinct from anxiety and depression, and they contribute uniquely to the impairment suffered by these individuals.

Second, the 10% to 15% of bereaved people who suffer persistent severe grief reactions experience marked psychological, social, health or occupational impairment. This can include other psychological problems (such as depression, suicidality, substance abuse), poor health behaviours (increased tobacco use), medical disorders (high blood pressure, elevated cancer rates, increased cardiovascular disorder) and functional disability.

Third, prolonged grief has been shown across a wide range of cultures, including non-western settings, as well as across the lifespan.

Fourth, and importantly, whereas bereavement-related depression responds to antidepressants, grief reactions do not. In contrast, treatments specifically targeted towards the core symptoms of prolonged grief are effective in alleviating the condition, and more effective than treatments that target depression.

A major issue influencing the introduction of the new diagnosis is the requirement to identify bereaved people in need of appropriate mental health care and to ensure they receive appropriate treatment.

Studies have repeatedly shown that leaving this condition untreated will result in the affected people suffering marked psychological, medical and social problems. On the premise that up to 15% of bereaved people experience complicated grief, there are over 70,000 new cases of prolonged grief in the United States each year, representing a very significant public health issue.

A common concern is that many people presenting to health providers with grief are misdiagnosed with depression, and prescribed antidepressants. The available evidence indicates this will not assist recovery from prolonged grief.

Several studies have shown that cognitive behaviour therapy (CBT) is an effective intervention for prolonged grief. CBT is a talking therapy that typically gets the person to focus on memories of the death and the relationship in a structured way. They learn more adaptive ways of appraising the loss and their relationship with the deceased, and then develop strategies for re-engaging with other people and activities.

Although CBT does not alleviate all prolonged grief cases, it is the best treatment we currently have available.

The concerns about potentially medicalising grief reactions and over-diagnosis are justified, however the proposed criteria have sufficient safe-guards built in. By limiting the diagnosis to persistent severe reactions that extend beyond 12 months after the bereavement, only a minority of bereaved people will receive this new diagnosis.

Hopefully, people suffering this potentially debilitating condition will now be able to receive the right treatment to allow them to move on with their life.

*25 October 2012*

⇨ The above information is reprinted with kind permission from The Conversation. Please visit www.theconversation.com for further information.

# What it takes to truly heal after a death in your life – the right and the wrong of grief

It your goal is to live with, manage or cope with grief, then by all means there is no right or wrong way – read all the books or not, join bereavement groups or not, spend years in therapy or not, believe in the five stages or not. There are many different ways to live with grief so I guess there is no right or wrong.

But I'm not talking about living with grief. I am never talking about living with grief. I'm talking about healing from grief. And once you've healed there is no need to cope with, manage or live with grief... as there is no more grief. Only love.

So if true healing from grief is what you want (and if it's not then you are in the wrong place and talking to the wrong girl!) then I agree there are no right ways, as long as the path you are following will lead to healing.

My dear friends Tabitha Jayne and Leo Searle Hawkins have both healed completely and totally from grief. No pain, no grief – just love. And both have processes that are totally different to mine and totally different to each other, to help others get there. But all three of us live in the same space around death and get our clients to the same destination. There is no one right path to healing...as long as the path you are on is actually heading in a healing direction.

And this is where I disagree with the 'no right or wrong' thing and believe that there are wrong ways to deal with grief if you want to heal. If you don't then continue doing whatever

you like... but I know that isn't you. I know that you do want to heal. Or you wouldn't be here.

If you do wish to heal you need to let go of everything I mention in the text above. Let go of everything you've been told about grief – that it lasts forever, that it never goes away, that it is love, that it is connection, that it is memory, that there are five stages... or any stages of all – none of these things are true and these beliefs will be the massive barriers that stop you healing (just like they have stopped the people who told you them in the first place from healing).

Think of this like getting fit. It you decided you want to get fit, there isn't a right way (do yoga, or start running, or join a gym, or take up swimming, or join acrobatics, or pole dancing, etc. etc.) but there are wrong ways (sitting on the sofa for entire days in front of your computer in your trackies... like I'm doing right this second, not doing any exercise at all, joining a support group for people who want to get fit but only talk about it to each other and still don't do any exercise, watching endless yoga videos without any 'doing' or just reading fitness books but not taking action with them). When I say 'wrong' I mean that if getting fit is your goal then these practices won't get you to your goal. In fact they will take you further away.

I am yet to meet a single person who has totally healed from grief after a death who hadn't had to let go of all of their old un-useful ideas and beliefs and 'common sense' around grief to

get there. The same as getting fit – these old ideas and practices won't get you closer to healing. In fact they ensure you stay well away.

It might sounds hard to do – to drop all these beliefs – and I'll grant you that it takes some work... but it may just be easier than you imagine and all it has to start with is a question.

What if all I think I know about grief isn't true? What if all I think I know about grief isn't helping me heal? What if all I've been told about grief I no longer need to believe in?

What if it is possible to totally heal... and I just never knew it?

Take it from someone who has been there, down in the dark depths of grief, and who worked their way completely out of it... it is.

Much love,

Kristie

xx

*25 June 2014*

To read the blog in full please visit http://kristiewest.com/2014/06/25/what-it-takes-to-truly-heal-after-a-death-in-your-life-the-right-and-the-wrong-of-grief/

⇨ The above information is reprinted with kind permission from Kristie West, the G.R.I.E.F Specialist. Please visit www.kristiewest.com for further information.

# Ten tips on coping with pet loss

*By Moira Anderson Allen, M.Ed.*

Anyone who considers a pet a beloved friend, companion, or family member knows the intense pain that accompanies the loss of that friend. Following are some tips on coping with that grief, and with the difficult decisions one faces upon the loss of a pet.

## 1. Am I crazy to hurt so much?

Intense grief over the loss of a pet is normal and natural. Don't let anyone tell you that it's silly, crazy, or overly sentimental to grieve!

During the years you spent with your pet (even if they were few), it became a significant and constant part of your life. It was a source of comfort and companionship, of unconditional love and acceptance, of fun and joy. So don't be surprised if you feel devastated by the loss of such a relationship.

People who don't understand the pet/owner bond may not understand your pain. All that matters, however, is how you feel. Don't let others dictate your feelings: they are valid, and may be extremely painful. But remember, you are not alone: thousands of pet owners have gone through the same feelings.

## 2. What can I expect to feel?

Different people experience grief in different ways. Besides your sorrow and loss, you may also experience the following emotions:

Guilt may occur if you feel responsible for your pet's death – the 'if only I had been more careful' syndrome. It is pointless and often erroneous to burden yourself with guilt for the accident or illness that claimed your pet's life, and only makes it more difficult to resolve your grief.

Denial makes it difficult to accept that your pet is really gone. It's hard to imagine that your pet won't greet you when you come home, or that it doesn't need its evening meal. Some pet owners carry this to extremes, and fear their pet is still alive and suffering somewhere. Others find it hard to get a new pet for fear of being 'disloyal' to the old.

Anger may be directed at the illness that killed your pet, the driver of the speeding car, the veterinarian who 'failed' to save its life. Sometimes it is justified, but when carried to extremes, it distracts you from the important task of resolving your grief.

Depression is a natural consequence of grief, but can leave you powerless to cope with your feelings. Extreme depression robs you of motivation and energy, causing you to dwell upon your sorrow.

## 3. What can I do about my feelings?

The most important step you can take is to be honest about your feelings. Don't deny your pain, or your feelings of anger and guilt. Only by examining and coming to terms with your feelings can you begin to work through them.

You have a right to feel pain and grief! Someone you loved has died, and you feel alone and bereaved. You have a right to feel anger and guilt, as well. Acknowledge your feelings first, then ask yourself whether the circumstances actually justify them.

Locking away grief doesn't make it go away. Express it. Cry, scream, pound the floor, talk it out. Do what helps you the most. Don't try to avoid grief by not thinking about your pet; instead, reminisce about the good times. This will help you understand what your pet's loss actually means to you.

Some find it helpful to express their feelings and memories in poems, stories or letters to the pet. Other strategies include rearranging your schedule to fill in the times you would have spent with your pet; preparing a memorial such as a photo collage; and talking to others about your loss.

## 4. Who can I talk to?

If your family or friends love pets, they'll understand what you're going through. Don't hide your feelings in a misguided effort to appear strong and calm! Working through your feelings with another person is one of the best ways to put them in perspective and find ways to handle them. Find someone you can talk to about how much the pet meant to you and how much you miss it – someone you feel comfortable crying and grieving with.

If you don't have family or friends who understand, or if you need more help, ask your veterinarian or humane association to recommend a pet loss counsellor or support group. Check with your church or hospital for grief counselling. Remember, your grief is genuine and deserving of support.

## 5. When is the right time to euthanise a pet?

Your veterinarian is the best judge of your pet's physical condition; however, you are the best judge of the quality of your pet's daily life. If a pet has a good appetite, responds to attention, seeks its owner's company, and participates in play or family life, many owners feel that this is not the time. However, if a pet is in constant pain, undergoing difficult and stressful treatments that aren't helping greatly, unresponsive to affection, unaware of its surroundings, and uninterested in life, a caring pet owner will probably choose to end the beloved companion's suffering.

Evaluate your pet's health honestly and unselfishly with your veterinarian. Prolonging a pet's suffering in order to prevent your own ultimately helps neither of you. Nothing can make this decision an easy or painless one, but it is truly the final act of love that you can make for your pet.

## 6. Should I stay during euthanasia?

Many feel this is the ultimate gesture of love and comfort you can offer your pet. Some feel relief and comfort themselves by staying. They were able to see that their pet passed peacefully and without pain, and that it was truly gone. For many, not witnessing the death (and not seeing the body) makes it more difficult to accept that the pet is really gone. However, this can be traumatic,

and you must ask yourself honestly whether you will be able to handle it. Uncontrolled emotions and tears – though natural – are likely to upset your pet.

Some clinics are more open than others to allowing the owner to stay during euthanasia. Some veterinarians are also willing to euthanise a pet at home. Others have come to an owner's car to administer the injection. Again, consider what will be least traumatic for you and your pet, and discuss your desires and concerns with your veterinarian. If your clinic is not able to accommodate your wishes, request a referral.

## 7. What do I do next?

When a pet dies, you must choose how to handle its remains. Sometimes, in the midst of grief, it may seem easiest to leave the pet at the clinic for disposal. Check with your clinic to find out whether there is a fee for such disposal. Some shelters also accept such remains, though many charge a fee for disposal.

If you prefer a more formal option, several are available. Home burial is a popular choice, if you have sufficient property for it. It is economical and enables you to design your own funeral ceremony at little cost. However, city regulations usually prohibit pet burials, and this is not a good choice for renters or people who move frequently.

To many, a pet cemetery provides a sense of dignity, security, and permanence. Owners appreciate the serene surroundings and care of the grave site. Cemetery costs vary depending on the services you select, as well as upon the type of pet you have. Cremation is a less expensive option that allows you to handle your pet's remains in a variety of ways: bury them (even in the city), scatter them in a favourite location, place them in a columbarium, or even keep them with you in a decorative urn (of which a wide variety are available).

Check with your veterinarian, pet shop, or phone directory for options available in your area. Consider your living situation, personal and religious values, finances, and future plans when making your decision. It's also wise to make such plans in advance, rather than hurriedly in the midst of grief.

## 8. What should I tell my children?

You are the best judge of how much information your children can handle about death and the loss of their pet. Don't underestimate them, however. You may find that, by being honest with them about your pet's loss, you may be able to address some fears and misconceptions they have about death.

Honesty is important. If you say the pet was 'put to sleep', make sure your children understand the difference between death and ordinary sleep. Never say the pet 'went away', or your child may wonder what he or she did to make it leave, and wait in anguish for its return. That also makes it harder for a child to accept a new pet. Make it clear that the pet will not come back, but that it is happy and free of pain.

Never assume a child is too young or too old to grieve. Never criticise a child for tears, or tell them to 'be strong' or not to feel sad. Be honest about your own sorrow; don't try to hide it or children may feel required to hide their grief as well. Discuss the issue with the entire family, and give everyone a chance to work through their grief at their own pace.

## 9. Will my other pets grieve?

Pets observe every change in a household, and are bound to notice the absence of a companion. Pets often form strong attachments to one another, and the survivor of such a pair may seem to grieve for its companion. Cats grieve for dogs, and dogs for cats.

You may need to give your surviving pets a lot of extra attention and love to help them through this period. Remember that, if you are going to introduce a new pet, your surviving pets may not accept the newcomer right away, but new bonds will grow in time. Meanwhile, the love of your surviving pets can be wonderfully healing for your own grief.

## 10. Should I get a new pet right away?

Generally, the answer is no. One needs time to work through grief and loss before attempting to build a relationship with a new pet. If your emotions are still in turmoil, you may resent a new pet for trying to 'take the place' of the old – for what you really want is your old pet back. Children in particular may feel that loving a new pet is 'disloyal' to the previous pet.

When you do get a new pet, avoid getting a 'look-alike' pet, which makes comparisons all the more likely. Don't expect your new pet to be 'just like' the one you lost, but allow it to develop its own personality. Never give a new pet the same name or nickname as the old. Avoid the temptation to compare the new pet to the old one: it can be hard to remember that your beloved companion also caused a few problems when it was young!

A new pet should be acquired because you are ready to move forward and build a new relationship – rather than looking backward and mourning your loss. When you are ready, select an animal with whom you can build another long, loving relationship – because this is what having a pet is all about!

⇨ The above information is reprinted with kind permission from Pet Loss. Please visit www.pet-loss.net for further information.

© 2014 Moira Anderson Allen

# What is a Death Cafe?

*Death Cafe*

At a Death Cafe people, often strangers, gather to eat cake, drink tea and discuss death.

Our objective is 'to increase awareness of death with a view to helping people make the most of their (finite) lives'.

A Death Cafe is a group-directed discussion of death with no agenda, objectives or themes. It is a discussion group rather than a grief support or counselling session.

Our Death Cafe franchises are always offered:

⇨ On a not-for-profit basis

⇨ In an accessible, respectful and confidential space

⇨ With no intention of leading people to any conclusion, product or course of action

⇨ Alongside refreshing drinks and nourishing food – and cake!

If you're interested in holding a Death Cafe please see our how-to guide on our website.

Death Cafe is a 'social franchise'. This means that people who sign up to our guide and principles can use the name Death Cafe, post events to this website and talk to the press as an affiliate of Death Cafe.

Death Cafes have spread quickly across Europe, North America and Australasia. As of today, we have offered 895 Death Cafes since September 2011. If ten people came to each one that would be 8,950 participants. We've established both that there are people who are keen to talk about death and that many are passionate enough to organise their own Death Cafe.

The Death Cafe model was developed by Jon Underwood and Sue Barsky Reid, based on the ideas of Bernard Crettaz.

Death Cafe has no staff and is run on a voluntary basis by Jon Underwood in Hackney, East London. Also Lizzy Miles who ran the first Death Cafe in the US and Megan Mooney who runs the Death Cafe Facebook page have played a significant role in Death Cafe's development.

We remain energised by the amazing quality of the dialogue at our events and are overwhelmed by the interest we have received.

People often ask why we doing this. Everyone has their own reasons for getting involved in Death Cafe.

## Our history

In 2010 Jon Underwood decided to develop a series of projects about death, one of which was to focus on talking about death. In November Jon read about the work of Bernard Crettaz in *The Independent* newspaper. Inspired by Bernard's work, Jon immediately decided to use a similar model for his own project, and Death Cafe was born.

The first Death Cafe in the UK was offered in Jon's house in Hackney, East London in September 2011. It was facilitated by psychotherapist Sue Barsky Reid, Jon's mum. It was a wonderful occasion. We went on to offer Death Cafes in a range of places including funky cafes, people's houses, cemeteries, a yurt and the Royal Festival Hall.

Jon and Sue Barsky Reid produced a guide to running your own Death Cafe, based around the methodology Sue developed. This was published in February 2012 and first person to pick it up outside of the UK was Lizzy Miles in Columbus, Ohio. Subsequently, hundreds of people have worked with us to provide Death Cafes across the globe.

Death Cafe has received some lovely media coverage including:

⇨ Death Be Not Decaffeinated: Over Cup, Groups Face Taboo *New York Times* (front page!)

⇨ Death Cafes Breathe Life Into Conversations About Dying NPR

⇨ The death cafe movement: Tea and mortality *The Independent*

⇨ 'Death cafes' normalize a difficult, not morbid, topic USA Today

We are currently working to establish a real Death Cafe in London.

Death Cafe is also:

⇨ On Facebook: facebook.com/deathcafe

⇨ On Twitter: @deathcafe

⇨ The above information is reprinted with kind permission from Impermanence. Please visit www.deathcafe.com for further information.

# Let's bring back mourning clothes

**By Jana Riess**

The first time I ever heard of mourning clothes was when I read *Gone with the Wind* in the eighth grade. The novel presents a fair amount of hand-wringing about the funeral mores of polite society. How long should the widowed young Scarlett wear black? Are those rules relaxed in wartime? And is it really proper for Scarlett to dance in her widow's garb even if it's in support of the war effort and Melanie Hamilton Wilkes has given it two thumbs up?

As a teenager I had no cultural context for mourning clothes, and assumed that wearing nothing but black for up to a year must have been the worst kind of stigma. But as an adult I have had cause to reconsider.

The purpose of mourning clothes wasn't to stigmatise death or, by contrast, to enshrine it (although the Victorians – led by their namesake queen, who dressed in black for 40 years after the death of her beloved husband – certainly did elevate mourning to an art form).

No, the purpose of the all-black fashion regimen was to give the bereaved survivors some much-needed cultural latitude. The clothes they wore practically screamed, 'The following person requires a wide berth. Don't take it personally if she is distracted, or he is brusque. It's not about you.'

Having just lost my mother last month, I crave this kind of Mourner's EZ Pass, this allowance to not have to 'move on' as soon as earth is scattered on a casket. In America today, we wear black to the funeral (and sometimes not even then, alas) and then are expected to dress as if nothing has happened, as if our world has not just shattered to pieces. Our grief is supposed to recede into something politely private and unobtrusive.

But I don't want my grief to be private and unobtrusive; I want my grief to be understood without my having to constantly explain it. Everything now feels too loud and too bright. When the checker at the grocery store asks me idly how I am doing, how can I refrain from grabbing the neck of his too-cheerful smock and hissing that I've had better days, thank you very much?

If I announced, 'My mother just died!' he would no doubt be cluckingly sympathetic. Most people are kind when presented with raw grief.

But I don't want to have to tell him. I want him to simply see and know.

Our ancestors understood this, and in fact kept up the traditions of mourning dress until the 20th century. The question for them was not whether someone would don mourning attire after the death of an immediate family member, but what kind and for how long. In graduate school I knew someone researching the fact that major department stores customarily had an entire mourning department well into the 1920s. I imagine this was the mourner's one-stop-shopping haven; a grieving person could pick up the necessary black shoes, hat, gloves, or armbands in a single shopping trip, attended by discreetly hushed sales clerks.

Mourning clothes gave people permission to take time to grieve. If society judged Scarlett O'Hara harshly for dancing with Rhett Butler while her most recent husband was barely cold in his grave, well, it also gave those who felt truly devastated by death broad cultural permission to wallow for an entire year.

And damn it, I need to wallow. I am betrayed by the very notion that the world outside my window dares to go on as usual. I ought to dress accordingly.

*Jana Riess is the author of* Flunking Sainthood: A Year of Breaking the Sabbath, Forgetting to Pray, and Still Loving My Neighbor, *and a blogger for Religion News Service.*

*25 February 2013*

# Remembering

'**G**rief is not about forgetting the person who has died, but about finding ways to remember them. Remembering brings healing. When someone dies, our feelings for them and memories of them stay alive and active inside us. We need to find ways of expressing those feelings so that we can move on in our lives,' says Julia Samuel, an experienced bereavement counsellor.

When you lose someone important in your life, you may fear you will be unable to conjure up all the happy memories of your life with them. This fear is very common. By taking an active part in creating ways of remembering, you can turn those memories into your most prized possessions. This is as true for children as it is for adults.

Finding ways to remember can help you. There is no right way or wrong way of remembering, nor is this a question of seeking perfection in whatever you have chosen to create. At its best, this process is a deeply personal expression of love for the special person in your life who has died but who lives on in your memories.

## The funeral

The funeral is a way of saying goodbye and is also an occasion to look back on and to remember. Because of its importance do make sure you know about the wide range of choices which are available these days. A funeral service no longer needs to follow a fixed format. You can create a ceremony that really expresses the spirit of the person who has died. Take time to consider the options. Whatever you decide, the memory of a beautiful service that felt absolutely right will bring you comfort in the future.

## Visiting the grave

This can be a way of 'visiting' the person who has died. For many people it is a chance to put the rest of the world aside. You may find that telling them your news, expressing your feelings to them and showing your love through flowers and other gifts becomes an integral part of your mourning.

## A memory box

You can make or buy a special box in which to put precious possessions. These could include letters or cards from friends or dried flowers from the funeral. You could also put into the box treasured things which belonged to the person who has died such as diaries or letters. Ready-made memory boxes often have sections for different keepsakes and a clear plastic cover on the lid for a photograph.

## A remembrance book

Creating a book in memory of the person who has died can be a healing process. Include photographs, poems, letters or your own thoughts. In the future the book will bring your memories back to life.

## A journal

Writing a diary of your grieving process is useful for a number of reasons. The writing itself is cathartic: putting your feelings into words can help to release some of the pain. Later, you will be able to look back on how you felt and to realise that however bad it was, you survived. That knowledge can help you to realise that whatever you are going through now will also pass. How you use the journal is, of course, up to you – some people sketch, others write down memories, others pour out feelings, yet others do a combination of all of these. You may choose to fill your journal with something entirely original.

## Artwork

If you like sewing, stitching a sampler and framing it can be a lovely option. You could paint a picture and frame that. Making anything in the memory of the person who has died connects you to them and gives you something to treasure.

## A candle

Lighting a candle and reading a special prayer or poem can be a simple but powerful way of commemorating an anniversary.

## A special walk

One family sent a beautifully illustrated leaflet about a special walk in memory of a little girl. The leaflet showed the route, described the girl and invited anyone who was interested to go on the walk. It was about two miles long, followed roads, went through a wood and ended by a river. Along the way were little hand-carved commemorative plaques with a few lines of a poem or a line drawing. You could create your own special walk.

## Planting trees or shrubs

Some people plant a tree or a shrub and have a commemorative plaque set up beside it as a way of remembering. Choose a hardy shrub or tree and make sure you plant it in a place that you will always be able to visit. If you have no place of your own to plant a tree, you may be able to get permission to plant one in a park or other public area.

## In memory of...

Some families, particularly when a child has died, like to create a charity or a scholarship in their memory – a living memorial to the person. This can be a way of healing the wounds of the person's death. You can invest in a cure for the disease that led to their death, develop their field of interest or continue their work.

## Remembrance service

Many organisations like Child Bereavement UK, Cruse (www.crusebereavementcare.org.uk) and Sands (Stillbirth and Neonatal Death Charity – www.uk-sands.org) hold national annual memorial services. Hospitals often hold a remembrance service each year.

You can organise your own service for your hospital or an organisation connected with the person who has died. These services are usually very beautiful and enormously appreciated. There is something deeply moving about a group of people from different backgrounds and with different stories coming together in one place to remember the special people in their lives. The service itself is often non-denominational and simple with a few prayers, poems and hymns, followed by the lighting of candles at the alter by members of the congregation.

For some people who have really moved forward in their lives, this service can be the only time they are able to put aside to remember, to feel the sadness again and to be enriched by the memories.

⇨ The above information is reprinted with kind permission from Child Bereavement UK. Please visit www.childbereavement.org.uk for further information.

*© Written by Julia Samuel for Child Bereavement UK*

# Ten ways to remember people on special days

## ... maybe their birthday or the anniversary of their death.

1.  Take a special card to their grave – or to where their ashes were buried or scattered

2.  Tie a card or a special message to a helium balloon and let it soar into the sky

3.  Blow some bubbles and send them your love on the wind

4.  Plant some bulbs or a shrub in a place that holds special memories of the person who has died – what was their favourite colour?

5.  Have their favourite meal – Risotto? Roast dinner? Curry?

6.  Listen to their favourite music

7.  Begin to make a memory box in which to keep things that remind you of the person – photos, shells, holiday snaps, glasses, etc.

8.  Make or buy a new frame for your favourite photograph

9.  Ask other people for their memories of the person who died and begin to compile their 'life story'

10. Write them a letter or a poem or a song. Maybe you could start with something like 'If you came back for just five minutes, I'd tell you...'

⇨ The above information is reprinted with kind permission from Winston's Wish. Please visit www.winstonswish.org.uk for further information.

*© Winston's Wish 2014*

# Facebook, death and memorialisation

*By Daniel Miller*

Alongside my ethnographic research in The Glades I have now been working for over a year alongside The Hospice of St Francis. When I am in the UK I try to spend a day a week interviewing their patients who are mainly terminal cancer patients. I was delighted to hear this winter that the wonderful hospice director Dr Ros Taylor was awarded an MBE in this year's honours list. My intention in working for the hospice was a concern that a project of this size should also have an applied or welfare aspect where we could see the direct benefit. The initial work was simply an attempt to see how the hospice could benefit from new media. The report was published on my website, but once I was working with them I realised that in a way the hospice was the clearest example of what the whole team have endeavoured to demonstrate through this blog.

The hospice movement represents no kind of technical or medical advancement. It is entirely the product of a transformation in collective consciousness. Previously it was assumed that when people knew they were dying this was tantamount to a stage in merely their withdrawal from the world. We talk about 'investing in our children' as though there were long-term financial assets. The same logic would condemn the dying as of limited value. The hospice movement was all about saying that knowing someone is terminal should be seen as an opportunity. It is no longer a medical issue, they will not be cured, instead we can concentrate on their quality of life and make this stage of life, since that is what it is, as enjoyable and fulfilling as it could be. Everything that Dr Taylor says and does demonstrates this, as does my colleague in this research, Kimberley McLaughlin, a senior manager of the hospice.

On reflection this is perhaps our single most important finding also as anthropologists of social media. People become fixated on the technological advances of new media. What each device can now be capable of – the latest app or smartphone or platform. These certainly feature throughout our work. But the vast majority of our blog posts are not about that. Instead they describe changes in the same collective consciousness: the social uses that people creatively imagine for these media as part of their lives.

The two issues come together in my observations of Facebook in relation to death and memorialisation. One of my early informants was a woman who felt that she wanted to use the experience of terminal cancer to help educate the wider world about her experience. A subject people tend to avoid but need to gain a better understanding of. I last saw her six days before she died and she was quite clear that using Facebook as almost a daily blog had enabled her to do just that. I am hoping (if I obtain the funding) to make a film based on her and other patients who have used Facebook in this manner.

I would be equally positive about the ways people have found to use Facebook in memorialisation and grief. Previously we have tended to use highly formal and religious institutionalised frames for dealing with death. As I argued in my book *Tales From Facebook*, this was out of synch with changes in our notion of the authenticity of the individual. Where once we took formal posed pictures, now we like to capture images that seem spontaneous, informal and thereby more 'real' to us. Similarly we needed a form of memorialisation that contained this element of personalisation and immediacy. People on Facebook can put both serious and jokey memories and do so at a time of their choosing. I find these sites poignant and effective. I don't find other social media sites, such as Twitter or Instagram, as having the same potential, so I hope we retain this capacity of Facebook.

But the point is that the inventors of Facebook were certainly not thinking about its relationship to death or memorialisation. Rather, as in the case of the invention of the hospice movement, this reflects a change in our collective imagination in what we could potentially do in relation to death and grief. This is why we argue it is anthropology rather than more tech-driven studies of new media that are most suited to understanding what social media actually become. Most of these reports reflect not the technological potential, but the imaginative realisation of social media.

*13 March 2014*

⇨ The above information is reprinted with kind permission from UCL. Please visit www. blogs.ucl.ac.uk for further information.

# White lines, white crosses: the controversy of roadside memorials

*By M. Gillies*

After the death of Diana, Princess of Wales, the Pont de L'Alma road tunnel in Paris (the site of her death) became a roadside memorial to the People's Princess. An avalanche of flowers and wreaths soon became an auspicious sight at both Kensington and Buckingham Palace as the public showed the outpour of their grief for a woman whom they held in high-esteem – the Flame of Liberty located at the Pont de L'Alma's north end became the unofficial memorial to her legacy and a roadside memorial marker to her tragedy. Since that day, the urban shrine has only grown in popularity.

Today, it isn't uncommon to see highways/freeways and major roads lined with white-crosses, flowers, trinkets and messages – these are what have become known as spontaneous shrines in honour of those who had died in a road crash. While their history can be traced back to ancient Greece, when shrines built to pagan gods were constructed along well-travelled paths for evening travellers to take a brief moment of rest and prayerful reflection, the usage of roadside memorial markers has been recognised as a new phenomenon.

Taking its tradition from early Hispanic settlers of the Southwestern United States, the contemporary roadside memorial evolved from Hispanic funerary processions known as *descanso*. As the funeral procession carried the coffin from the church to a graveyard, bearers would be inclined to take a moment of rest. It would be during this time that the bearers would place a cross to mark the spot where the coffin was set down in memory of the event – in a similar vein, the practice of roadside memorials has become a commemoration of the last place a person was alive before their fatal injury, and they are appearing in greater numbers.

From simple to elaborate, makeshift or permanent, roadside memorials have become public markers of private trauma and grief. They tell the story of a life taken too soon – they have become personal statements bearing witness to a life lost and they act as a memento to others both to offer a moment of quiet reflection on the significance of the fragility of a person's life, and as a heeded warning of dangers we have become too complacent in noticing.

Even New York City has seen an influx with memorial markers lining the streets, in the form of Ghost Bikes to commemorate both cyclists and pedestrians who have

been killed on New York City streets – an initiative created by The Street Memorial Project.

However, while these memorials are usually private rather than public, there are laws that can restrict roadside memorials from being created. But that isn't the only thing that is standing in the way of the contemporary roadside memorial. In fact, highway officials in the United States have claimed that too many roadside memorials can become distracting and dangerous – these complaints often stemming in regards to the permanent or near permanent shrines. But it isn't the wreaths or flowers being placed on the anniversary of an accident that are stirring up the controversy, but rather the religious messages being conveyed through the use of a cross.

In recent news, many atheist activists have petitioned to have states regulate the use of roadside memorials, ensuring that all religious symbology be removed and restricted from being placed on state property. But it isn't only in the United States where roadside memorials have been a controversial topic.

Russian officials have been addressing the usage of roadside memorials for car crash victims for some time now, and have even made a federal law which can count setting roadside memorials, wreaths or crosses as an administrative offence, further implementing a ban on roadside memorials and eliminating current ones.

Meanwhile in South Africa, warnings have been given that the practice of erecting a roadside memorial could have equally devastating and fatal consequences for motorists as the South African National Roads Agency states that roadside memorials, including plaques, crosses and wreaths can pose a safety threat to other motorists travelling the roads through distractions.

As the state of Colorado pointed out during a court matter involving roadside memorials, it was said, because it is public ground and not private, and, further, no authorisation or permission was given to place a memorial on state property, it is then seen as abandoned property.

While the primary purpose of a roadside memorial is to mark the

death of a loved one in a tragic incident, encouraging awareness of potential dangers and further giving an outlet for loved ones to grieve, states like Massachusetts, Wisconsin and Colorado have banned the use of such memorials, while California requires residents to pay a state fee of $1,000.

When it comes to roadside memorials, because each state, city and country imposes different laws for the use of roadside memorials, it is often best to first check with the city by-laws on the regulations of erecting a roadside memorial. However, with many officials and citizens deeming them inappropriate for public property, it has been recommended that any kind of memorial be placed only on public property.

⇨ The above information is reprinted with kind permission from mysendoff.com. Please visit www.mysendoff.com for further information.

# Way to go: when will you die, how and with what support?

**THE CONVERSATION**

*An article from The Conversation.*

*By Katherine Sleeman, Clinical Lecturer in Palliative Medicine at King's College London*

Every year around half a million people die in England. The success of medicine over the past decades has led to a sustained rise in the average human life expectancy: a third of children born today will live to be 100 years old. However, it does not follow that fewer people are dying. In fact, the annual number of deaths in England has begun to rise and is projected to continue to do so for at least the next 20 years.

## How will you die?

What will the trajectory of our final deterioration be like? For around a fifth of us, our deaths will be sudden, and unpredictable – from a large stroke or an accident, for example. A further fifth of us are likely to die from cancer, and will live with relatively good

SO MANY WONDERFUL MEMORIES.

WHICH WE'LL ALWAYS HAVE.

IN MEMORY

physical function until quite close to death, when there is usually a relatively linear deterioration over weeks. The rest – the majority of us – will live with and die from chronic medical problems such as heart failure, kidney failure and dementia, and our final days, weeks and months will be characterised by relapses and remissions against a background of a slowly progressive deterioration in physical function.

## Palliative care

Palliative care is a philosophy of care for people who are approaching the ends of their lives, where the goal is to improve the patient's comfort and quality of life, rather than trying to extend or increase its quantity. The word palliative comes from the Latin *palliare* meaning 'to cloak' and palliative care focuses on finding out what the worst problems for the patient and their family are, and to then improve them.

Part of the focus of palliative care is on relieving physical symptoms, which are common (though not universal) in people who are dying. More than a third of dying people will experience pain. Effective treatment depends on identifying the likely cause of it. For many types of pain, opioids such as morphine sulphate are the mainstay of treatment. It is important for patients to realise that taking opioids in the right doses for their pain will not cause them to become addicted, or to die more quickly.

A principle of palliative care is that only medication which has the aim of improving comfort is given to people who are thought to be dying. Drugs with longer-term benefits (such as cholesterol-lowering drugs) are usually stopped. Medicines can be given by mouth, or in other forms such as injections or infusions under the skin if the patient finds swallowing difficult.

While assessment and treatment of physical symptoms is a large part of palliative care, it is also essential to address psychological, social and spiritual needs. Cicely Saunders, who founded the modern palliative care movement in the 1960s, defined the concept of Total Pain, suffering that encompasses not just physical but also social, psychological and spiritual dimensions. Therefore, in order to control pain in the dying it is necessary to explore these dimensions. Questions such as: 'How do you make sense of the future?', 'Where do you find your strength?' and 'What is most important to you?' are often useful.

Cicely Saunders said: 'How we die remains in the memory of those who live on.'

*23 July 2014*

⇨ The above information is reprinted with kind permission from The Conversation. Please visit www.theconversation.com for further information.

## When do you know it's the end?

How do we know when to 'switch' to palliative care? How do we know when a person is dying? The last weeks of life for most people are characterised by a progressive physical decline, frailty, lethargy, worsening mobility, reduced oral intake, and little or no response to medical interventions. However, these changes can be subtle. In people with frailty and dementia, the dying phase can be difficult to distinguish because patients can live for a long time with a very poor level of function.

It is therefore important to provide palliative care in parallel with, rather than in series with, other medical care. This will include having sensitive conversations with the patient and their carers about their wishes and preferences for the future, in anticipation of their deterioration. For example, many patients would prefer to die at home rather than in hospital and it is essential to explore such preferences while the patient remains well enough to travel.

These conversations can be hard for healthcare professionals, whose training equips them for saving lives, and for whom death is often viewed as failure. Both the doctor and the patient may view talking about death as an admission of defeat. But however uncomfortable these conversations are, the danger of avoiding them is a medicalised death, with more suffering for the patient, and more distress in bereavement for their carers. As

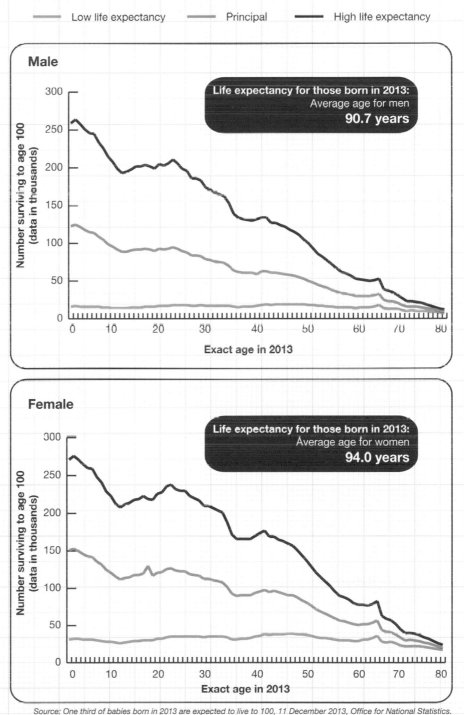

**Projected numbers of people surviving to their 100th birthday by their age in 2013, All variants, UK**

Low life expectancy — Principal — High life expectancy

**Male**

Number surviving to age 100 (data in thousands)

Life expectancy for those born in 2013:
Average age for men
**90.7 years**

Exact age in 2013

**Female**

Number surviving to age 100 (data in thousands)

Life expectancy for those born in 2013:
Average age for women
**94.0 years**

Exact age in 2013

Source: One third of babies born in 2013 are expected to live to 100, 11 December 2013, Office for National Statistics.

# What are the top causes of death by age and gender?

*ONS looks at leading causes of deaths registered in England and Wales, 2012.*

Heart disease was the biggest cause of death in 2012, killing over 64,000 people, followed by dementia and Alzheimer's disease, which caused more than 43,000 deaths, and cerebrovascular diseases which were responsible for more than 35,000 deaths. In 2012, 80% of men and 88% of women who died were aged 65 or over. The leading cause of death for men was heart disease (15.6%) and the leading cause for women was dementia and Alzheimer's disease (11.5%).

## One in 1,000 deaths were among children aged one to four in 2012

Around one in 1,000 deaths in 2012 were among children age one to four years old. The leading cause of death at this age was congenital malformations, deformations and chromosomal abnormalities (14% of boys, 16% of girls). These conditions are usually present at birth or develop shortly after, and include congenital heart defects.

These conditions were also the leading cause of death for girls aged between five and 19, accounting for 7% of deaths. Brain cancers, lymphoid cancers (including leukaemia) and land transport accidents each accounted for 6% of deaths to five- to 19-year-old girls, while the leading cause of death for boys of the same age was land transport accidents. Over three-quarters of all road traffic deaths occur among men. Worldwide, males under the age of 25 are almost three times more likely to be killed in a car crash than females of the same age.

## Suicide and poisoning leading cause of death for 20–34-year-olds

Suicide and injury/poisoning of undetermined intent were the leading cause of death for 20–34-year-olds, for 26% of men and 13% of women. Factors that could lead to these deaths include: traumatic experiences, lifestyle choices such as drug or alcohol misuse, job insecurity and relationship problems.

## Breast cancer leading cause of death for 35–49-year-old women

Suicide remains the leading cause of death for men up to the age of 49, accounting for 13% of deaths to men aged 35–49. Breast cancer is the leading cause of death among women in this age group, accounting for 15% of deaths. However, it is the leading cause because women in this age group are relatively healthy and are therefore less likely to die of other causes. Breast cancer deaths in women aged 15–49 only account for around 10% of all female breast cancer deaths.

## Heart disease leading cause of death for men aged 50 and over

For people aged 50 and over, the leading causes of death for both men and women are long-term diseases and conditions. Cancer of the trachea, bronchus and lung is the number one cause for women aged 50–64, accounting for 12% of deaths in this group. Breast cancer is the second leading cause of death for 50–64-year-old women, accounting for 11% of deaths in this age group.

Heart diseases are the leading cause of death for men aged 50 and over, and for women aged 65 to 79 years, these diseases are usually caused by the build up of fatty deposits on the walls of the arteries around the heart. Lifestyle choices and other conditions can lead to heart disease such as: smoking, high cholesterol, high blood pressure and diabetes. Heart disease was also the second leading cause of death for women over 80.

## Dementia and Alzheimer's leading cause of death for women over 80

For women over 80, dementia and Alzheimer's disease was the leading cause of death, accounting for 16% of female deaths in that age group and 11.5% of all female deaths in 2012. Dementia and Alzheimer's disease was the second leading cause of death for men in this age group. Alzheimer's disease is the most common cause of dementia. Deaths from dementia and Alzheimer's disease are increasing as people live longer, with women living longer than men.

## Where can I find out more about leading causes of death statistics?

If you'd like to find out more about the latest mortality statistics, please read our latest release. If you have any comments or suggestions, we'd like to hear them! Please e-mail us at: vsob@ons.gsi.gov.uk.

*12 December 2013*

⇨ The above information is reprinted with kind permission from the Office for National Statistics. Please visit www.ons.gov.uk for further information.

© *Crown copyright 2014*

# Why babies die

*Each year in the UK over 6,500 babies die just before, during or soon after birth. That's 17 babies every day.*

'The question about why your baby died never really goes away. For some parents there's a definite cause but for many there isn't and it can be a source of deep sadness and anxiety. We are working at Sands to help promote both prevention strategies and a set of research priorities that'll answer the questions so many parents are left with.' Janet Scott, Head of Research and Prevention.

## Stillbirth

Stillbirth is the death of a baby before or during birth after 24 or more weeks of pregnancy.

### How often does it happen?

11 babies are stillborn every day in the UK.[1]

Contrary to common perception stillbirth is not so rare a tragedy: one in 200 pregnancies ends in stillbirth.[2]

Stillbirth is around 15 times more common than cot death. Around 4,200 babies are stillborn every year in the UK, compared to over 250 babies who die every year as a result of sudden infant death (known commonly as cot death).[3]

In the last 20 years the decline in stillbirth rates which accompanied advances in maternity care has slowed and halted. UK rates of stillbirth today are the same as in the late 1990s.[4]

More than 30% of stillbirths happen at term (after 37 weeks gestation), the age when a baby is preparing to start life outside the womb.[4]

There are as many stillbirths in the UK as there are deaths of children under the age of five. If we count all babies who are alive from 24 weeks of pregnancy onwards as children, about 75% of all child deaths occur in the womb or in the first week of life.[5]

The UK's stillbirth rate is largely unchanged from a decade ago. Other countries have managed to reduce their stillbirth rates in recent decades: in Norway and The Netherlands stillbirths have fallen by 50% and 40% respectively in the last 20 years. Authors of a *Lancet* paper on this issue conclude: 'The variation in stillbirth rates clearly shows that further reduction in stillbirth is possible in high-income countries.'[6]

### Possible causes

Many people think that stillbirths happen because of a developmental or genetic problem that means the baby could not survive. In fact, fewer than one in ten stillbirths is caused by what's known as a 'major congenital abnormality'. In a large number of stillbirths, the baby appears to be completely healthy.

Sometimes the mother has a condition that affects the pregnancy and sometimes there are major problems with the placenta or the umbilical cord.

For around one-third of babies, there is no clear cause for the death. For another third of stillbirths the baby was apparently healthy but was smaller than would be expected. In both cases, these stillbirths may be described as 'unexplained'.

### Placental problems

Researchers believe that some 'unexplained' stillbirths happen because the placenta, which joins the woman's and baby's blood systems, starts working less well. The deterioration may happen gradually, and may not be picked up by current routine antenatal monitoring.

It may mean the baby doesn't grow as well as it should because the blood and oxygen supply is compromised in some way. Around a third of stillborn babies have not reached their growth potential and poor growth or growth that starts

well and tails off during pregnancy, is a sign that a baby is at risk of stillbirth. If this is the case, the baby may also start to move less often.

Sands is funding research that asks whether encouraging women to be aware of their baby's movements and to tell their midwife promptly if their baby is not moving as it normally does could help reduce the number of stillbirths.

If you are pregnant and are concerned about your baby's movements please contact your midwife.

We are also funding research looking at scanning in the third trimester, which is aimed at improving methods for identifying babies who are not growing as they should.

### Other conditions

Stillbirth may also happen because of:

⇨ bleeding (haemorrhage) before or during labour

⇨ placenta abruption, which is when the placenta separates from the womb before the baby is born

⇨ pre-eclampsia, which causes high blood pressure in the mother

⇨ the umbilical cord slipping down through the entrance of the womb before the baby is born (known as cord prolapse) or wrapping around the baby's neck

⇨ intrahepatic cholestasis of pregnancy (ICP) or obstetric cholestasis, a liver disorder

⇨ a genetic problem

⇨ gestational diabetes, which is a type of diabetes that develops during pregnancy

⇨ infection (for a list of infections which cause stillbirth visit NHS Choices).

### Post-mortems

Parents of a stillborn baby will be asked whether they want their baby to have a post-mortem. A post-mortem can sometimes find the cause of the stillbirth; it can also help rule out some causes. This information may be helpful if families are planning future pregnancies.

## Neonatal death

A neonatal death is the death of a baby within the first four weeks of life.

### How often does it happen?

Six babies die neonatally every day in the UK.[7]

In 2011, 1,821 babies died within the first hours or days of their lives, and another 561 died at between one and four weeks.[7]

The number of babies who die in the neonatal period – within the first 28 days of birth – has fallen by 20% over the last decade, largely due to progress in caring for premature infants. However, it still remains the case that one in 300 babies dies in the first four weeks of life and around a quarter of these babies are born at term.[8]

### Possible causes

Many babies who die within the first four weeks of life have a congenital disorder or were born prematurely. In the remainder of cases the cause is unknown or due to potentially avoidable issues that have originated in pregnancy and during labour. Around 500 babies die every year because of a trauma or event during birth that was not anticipated or well managed. Some are stillborn and some die neonatally. Many of these deaths, when they occur at term, could be avoided with better care.

## References

1. Death Registration Summary Statistics 2011, Office for National Statistics; The Annual Report of the Registrar General Northern Ireland 2011; Scotland's Population 2011: The Registrar General's Annual Review of Demographic Trends, 157th Edition.

2. England and Wales' stillbirth rate of 5.2/1,000 means that one in 200 pregnancies after 24 weeks ends in stillbirth.

3. In 2010 in the UK, 287 babies died as a result of sudden infant death syndrome (SIDS); according to statistics from The Office of National Statistics (ONS), General Register Office for Scotland (GROS) and Northern Ireland Statistics and Research Agency (NISRA), compared to 4,110 stillbirths in the same year, making stillbirth more than ten times more common than SIDS.

4. Perinatal Mortality Report 2009, Centre for Maternal and Child Enquiries 2011.

5. Infant and Perinatal Mortality in England and Wales by social and biological factors, Office of National Statistics 2010.

6. V Flenady et al. Stillbirths: the way forward in high-income countries. *The Lancet* 2011, Vol. 377, Issue 9778, Pages 1703–1717.

7. Office for National Statistics 2013. Child mortality statistics: childhood, infant and perinatal, 2011.

8. Perinatal Mortality Report 2009, Centre for Maternal and Child Enquiries 2011.

⇨ The above information is reprinted with kind permission from SANDS (Stillbirth and Neonatal Death Society). Please visit www.uk-sands.org for further information.

*© 2014 Sands (Stillbirth and Neonatal Death Society)*

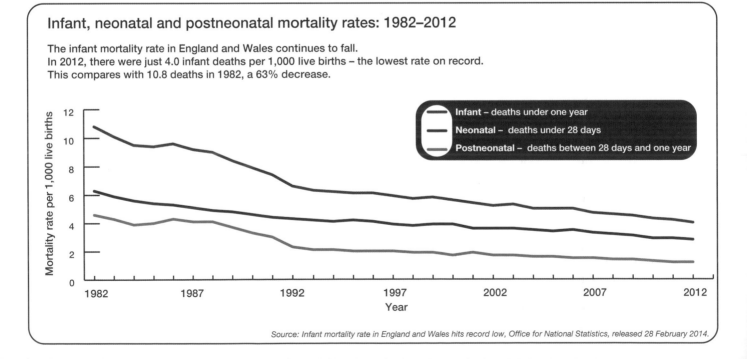

### Infant, neonatal and postneonatal mortality rates: 1982–2012

The infant mortality rate in England and Wales continues to fall.
In 2012, there were just 4.0 infant deaths per 1,000 live births – the lowest rate on record.
This compares with 10.8 deaths in 1982, a 63% decrease.

Infant – deaths under one year
Neonatal – deaths under 28 days
Postneonatal – deaths between 28 days and one year

*Source: Infant mortality rate in England and Wales hits record low, Office for National Statistics, released 28 February 2014.*

# Religion, faith and philosophy

**M**any people we talked to had a philosophy, faith or belief that made it easier for them to come to terms with terminal illness, death and dying. For example, some people firmly believed in Jesus Christ and life after death. One woman said that she was a 'true Christian believer' and had no fear of death. She was convinced that when someone dies the spirit leaves the body. When she felt very ill she said that death would be welcome. One man asserted that a belief in life after death could help him face death without fear. He finds it very important to pray for this belief.

Some people were unsure about the future, opting to keep an 'open mind'. One man hoped that there might be something 'behind the curtain', but found it hard to believe in life after death and wondered if he were simply 'clutching at straws'.

A woman with cancer of the kidney explained that although she described herself as a humanist, rather than a Christian, she found it comforting to know that others were praying for her. A man with mesothelioma also said that he wasn't religious, but was glad to know that others were praying for him, willing him to get better.

A woman with bowel cancer suggested that great comfort could be drawn from other religions too.

A few people said that they lost some of their faith when they became ill. For example, a Jewish man said he felt 'betrayed' and 'let down' by his religion because even though he had been told there was eternal life he had just found happiness in this life but couldn't appreciate it because he felt so ill.

A man with non-Hodgkin's lymphoma did not believe in life after death but he believed in a superior 'power'. He pointed out that if you have a family your genes continue even after death. He also stressed that in this life we can influence other people, and the way they live their lives, and thus leave a legacy in that way.

A woman with a strong moral sense that people should treat each other well, not because of religion but to 'make the world a better place' said that she could believe in spacemen or aliens more than she could believe in God. Another person said she hoped she had been a good influence on her family. She wanted to contribute to the healthtalk.org website partly because she saw it as a form of legacy she could be remembered by.

Most people who had no religious beliefs and didn't believe in life after death, recognised the comfort that others might draw from their religion and were careful not to offend them. However, one man noted the hypocrisy of some religious people and the harm that religion does in the world as a focus of conflict.

People who had seen death, either of people close to them or because of their work, often said that it helped them to see death as a natural process and nothing to be afraid of. One man said we should accept death as 'part of life'. Another man, a scientist and atheist, said that he wanted to be buried so that he could be 'recycled' to help whatever came along, 'whether the worms or whatever'. He certainly didn't want life hereafter but understood that people who had such beliefs found them comforting.

A woman whose father had died of motor neurone disease said that she found it hard to comfort him because his logical mind and background as a scientist prevented him from having a faith in any religion or a belief in an afterlife. She said that her father was very frightened of dying, but emotional and spiritual support was lacking. She had long conversations with him about death, and as a result her own religious faith was strengthened. She wanted to pass on a message to others that they should not be afraid of death.

Some people described themselves as 'fatalists'. A man with prostate cancer said he didn't believe in life after death, but accepted the situation, and suggested that there was no point in 'moping'; that it was important to have good quality life for as long as possible. Another man, who believed that fate was somehow genetic, said that he must have served his purpose on earth.

Older people suspected that they found death easier to accept than younger people, whether or not they had religious beliefs. As one person in her 70s said, her views about death being natural and expected would have been very different in her 20s or 30s.

*March 2012*

⇨ The above information is a summary of video interviews made by researchers of the University of Oxford as part of a larger project. To see the videos and learn more visit healthtalk.org and look for 'Living with Dying' under the A–Z index.

© *healthtalk.org*
© *University of Oxford*

# Overcoming obstacles: why is death a taboo?

*19-year-old Lucy, who has Ehlers-Danlos Syndrome, has been writing a blog since 2012 about what it is like to live with a life-limiting and life-threatening illness. Here we republish one of this inspiring young woman's recent posts on the importance of talking about death and of making the most of life. She also addresses misconceptions around hospices and palliative care.*

*By Lucy Watts*

Why is death such a taboo? It's the only thing guaranteed in life. Everyone knows they will die at some point or another. So why do we shy away from it? Whatever your beliefs, it will happen. Some people die before they're born, others die after a long, fulfilling life. The rest of us fit in somewhere in between.

Not many of us actually want to die. We might want the suffering to end, the pain to stop, for things to change; but when it comes down to it, very few of us actually want our lives to end. Dying is not a sin nor necessarily a bad thing. Why is it treated as so? Death should be as important as birth; there should be more emphasis placed on a good death as is placed on a good birth. I wonder if as much funding goes into death and dying as goes into bringing life into this world, when most hospices receive little-to-no funding from the Government?

We need to talk about death. We need to make our wishes known, discuss things like organ donation, what measures you want to be taken to save your life, whether you'd want to be kept alive by machines and what you want to happen after your death. We often don't talk about death until we are confronted by it; by a cancer, a terminal illness or life-limiting diagnosis. The same went for me. I never thought about death until we were told that my life will be limited. I was terrified of dying, mind you I still am, but I know those around me will endeavour to make my death as peaceful and painless as possible.

We've done my end of life plan, and we have talked many times about what I want. I've started writing down how I'd like my funeral to be, as I want it to be a celebration of my life. Partly I want to do it because it gives me a feeling of control. I struggle with the lack of control in my life, so the things I can control are very precious. The other reason I want to do it is because I want to reduce the stress on my family after I die; they don't have to think too much about what to do because they will know what I would like. As I said I like the things I can control; though I can't control my death, I certainly can make plans and make my wishes known.

I often wonder what will happen when I die. Will it be peaceful, will it be painful, will I be scared, will the people I want be with me, will I be at peace with the fact I am dying? There's so much to think and worry about. I am a worrier; always have been, always will be. I'm always worried about something. I worry about leaving my family and friends behind. How will they cope? Especially my mum and my sister. My mum has given up her life to keep me alive; what will she do when I'm no longer here? How will she cope without our lovely chats, walking the dog together and the laughter we share; laughter at times when most wouldn't know how to? How will Vicky continue with her life knowing she won't be able to share the highs and lows of life with her sister? Knowing I might not see her get married, meet her children or be able to share special moments together? Who will miss me? Will anything be different because of me? Will my life have meant something?

One of my biggest fears is that nothing will come out of my life; nothing will be different, better even, because of me. Everyone wants their life to mean something. Will I be lucky enough to have made an impact on the world? I hope so. My goal in life is to make a difference, something that I seem to be on the way to doing, but I want the impact to be as big and as good as it can. I don't want to be famous; I don't necessarily want people to know who I am and know what I did. I just want something to be different because of me. This extends to my wish for my organs to be donated if they can. Statistically you're more likely to need an organ than to be able to donate, and the same applies to me; I will probably need a bowel transplant at some point in the future, and I probably won't be able to donate my organs due to my conditions etc., but I want my organs and tissues to be donated where possible.

## Tough conversations

My mum and I have had to have some tough conversations; conversations no parent should have with their child. We have regular, hard discussions with my hospice nurse too. We talk about trivial things also, but many a night do we spend discussing serious, some heart-breaking, subjects. Subjects about life and death. We talk about my fears and my feelings, and occasionally we cry, though neither of us are criers. My mum has to watch me suffer day in, day out, see me reach some terrible lows and watch me deteriorate, losing more and more function as time goes on.

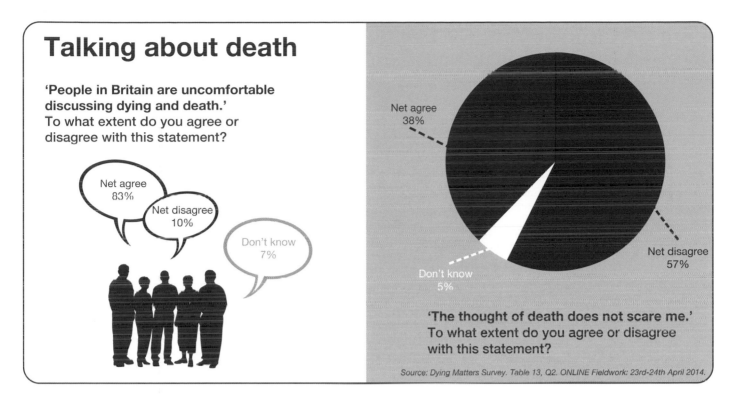

# Talking about death

**'People in Britain are uncomfortable discussing dying and death.'**
To what extent do you agree or disagree with this statement?

Net agree
83%

Net disagree
10%

Don't know
7%

Net agree
38%

Don't know
5%

Net disagree
57%

**'The thought of death does not scare me.'**
To what extent do you agree or disagree with this statement?

Source: Dying Matters Survey. Table 13, Q2. ONLINE Fieldwork: 23rd-24th April 2014.

She will most likely watch life leave me altogether; watch me breathe my last breath and slip away. It's supposed to be the other way round. No parent should have to bury their child.

## Misconceptions around hospices and palliative care

People seem to have such a fear when the words 'hospice' or 'palliative' are used. They immediately think death and dying; but it's so much more than that. It's about quality of life, symptom control, living well, laughter, fun and yes, also death. It's about your interests, your hobbies, achieving what you'd like to and being able to live for however long you have left. It's not about how long you've got; it's about how much you can fit into that time. You have to live quickly while you're dying. If you feel well enough: great, then do something. If you're not feeling so well: take it easy and save your energy for another time. Your priorities change. When time isn't on your side it's not about the latest gadgets, having the nicest house or impressing your friends, it's about getting all that you can out of life. It's the little things that mean the most. The smell after it rains;

watching the sun rise or set; seeing the sea; listening to your family and friends talk and laugh; decorating the tree at Christmas; hugs; being able to taste and eat food; anything that is usually trivial and things that we take for granted. You savour every moment you get.

The word palliative is somewhat comforting for me; it means I don't have to explain my pain or justify myself all the time, it means that someone will listen, it means my quality of life – rather than the length of my life – will be of the utmost importance. It means living well, relief from symptoms and reassurance. Palliative care is a word associated with dying, when in fact it couldn't be more opposite. It's about living well and symptom control in life and in death, not just about death itself.

Hospice has an even worse association with death than palliative care. Palliative care is for the dying, whereas hospices are where people go to die. However, they are also so much more than that. When I think of the word hospice, death is low down on my list. If you know anything about hospices, you'll know that they're not just a load of death beds. They help to improve the quality of your life, get on top of your symptoms, support your family, offer respite to give carers a break,

can give complementary therapies, be a step between hospital and home, AND can be a place to go at the end of your life for those who cannot be treated at home and those that do not want to die at home. The words laughter, love, fun, support, happiness, care, quality, family and comfort come to mind. I want to break the negative associations with hospices and palliative care. People need to realise they are not just about death, they're about living well in life and in death.

So be grateful for every day, make the most of it, make your wishes known and sign the organ donor register today rather than getting round to it another time. Nobody knows when they're going to die, so do it today, not tomorrow, as tomorrow might not come.

Read more of Lucy's writing at http:// lucyalexandria.blogspot.co.uk/

*4 March 2014*

⇨ The above Information is reprinted with kind permission from healthtalk.org. Please visit www.ehospice.com for further information.

© 2014 ehospice

# Thinking about death can make you value life more

*An article from The Conversation.*

THE CONVERSATION

*By Nathan Heflick, Research Associate in Psychology at the University of Kent*

**G**o ahead and contemplate your own mortality. How does it feel? Would you be surprised to learn that it can potentially improve your mental health to think about your death more often?

The Russian novelist Leo Tolstoy once pondered if there was any meaning in life that an awareness of death didn't undo or destroy. On the surface, this is undoubtedly true; everything and everyone we value, everything we cherish, could just vanish at any moment. As Sheldon Solomon, psychology professor at Skidmore College in New York, said, an awareness of our own death is potentially extremely distressing because it renders you aware that you are, ultimately, no more significant than food sources and animals, or as he put it: 'lizards and potatoes'.

It is also impossible to truly know what it is like to die. So here we are, as humans, in this predicament: we have this desire to live, but we ultimately know we will die, and we don't even know what it is like to experience what can often cause a high level of distress. The unknown is perhaps the scariest thing about it.

But there is another side to this. James Pennebaker, a psychology professor at the University of Texas, has conducted studies in which people wrote about deeply emotional – and hence often distressing – topics over the course of weeks or months. His work generally found that these writing exercises increased mental, and even physical, health. Of course, as he has noted, people often struggle with writing but nearly all of them reported that the experience was worthwhile and meaningful.

Dozens of studies across economics and psychology have found that when something (time included) is perceived as scarcer, it becomes more valuable. Writing about death, particularly writing repeatedly about death, makes salient the finitude of life, which is something we often take for granted and even actively avoid thinking about. It could then, theoretically, make people perceive that life is more valuable and something to be cherished.

Irvin Yalom, a clinical psychologist who deals with existential issues, has also written about how contemplating mortality on a deeper level can have positive psychological effects. He has argued specifically that people who accept and face death develop a more 'authentic' life in which their behaviour and goals more align with their values.

Along with colleagues, I've been conducting a few experiments to directly test the consequences of writing about mortality over time. Participants (college students) write about death or another aversive topic each day for one week, or they just reply to specific questions in an e-mail each day on which they have to spend five to ten minutes – one example they've been asked to reflect on is that if you're aware life is short and that you could die sooner than you think, how does it make you feel and how does it impact you in general?

After seven days they then complete a variety of quantitative measures that assess the extent to which they experienced positive and negative emotions, how they felt about themselves and how much they perceived their behaviour to be intrinsically motivated, in other words autonomous and free from external pressures.

Our research suggests that there are positive psychological effects to writing about mortality. Specifically, participants who are in the repeated death writing group have been reporting lower levels of depression, increased positive mood, increased self-esteem and increased intrinsic motivation.

There is also preliminary evidence that such writing might increase forgiveness towards people, including both reducing the desire for them to be harmed and increasing desire for reconciliation. Interestingly, many of these effects occur only in individuals who have moderate levels of depressive symptoms going into the study (though well below clinical levels). It appears then that the mildly depressed may benefit most from a deeper reflection on their own mortality.

German philosopher Martin Heidegger wrote about how death awareness (the 'nothing') enables us to shift to a mode where we simply appreciate that things are (the 'being there'), as opposed to worrying about how or what things are. Now experimental, quantitative research – arguably at the opposite end of the spectrum – is confirming the eloquent words of one of philosophy's greats.

*11 April 2014*

⇨ The above information is reprinted with kind permission from The Conversation. Please visit www.theconversation.com for further information.

# New study examines the language of dying

**The way in which people talk about death and dying is being analysed by researchers at Lancaster University in an innovative and far-reaching project.**

The £218,000 project, funded by the Economic and Social Research Council, brings together expertise from linguists, computer scientists and a health psychologist from the University's International Observatory on End of Life Care.

The 'Metaphor in End of Life Care' project focuses specifically on metaphors – words and phrases which describe one thing in terms of another. Illness, emotions, relationships and death are among the experiences for which people use metaphors to express, reflect and shape views, feelings, attitudes and needs.

The team is scrutinising 1.5 million words used by patients, family carers and healthcare professionals in a bid to improve communications for those nearing the end of their lives, in consultation with the Lancaster Research Partners' Forum – a group of local people with experience of research and of end-of-life care in the UK.

The project's principal investigator and Head of Linguistics and English Language Professor Elena Semino explained: 'Metaphors are often used to talk about experiences that are sensitive and emotional, or that might be taboo, and the choice of metaphor will reflect how we "see" or feel about those experiences.

'For example, if we talk about being ill with cancer in terms of a journey with milestones and crossroads, we may experience things differently than If we talk about it in terms of a battle – fighting an enemy, winning, or losing. The competitive, heroic element of battle metaphors can be motivating for some people but demoralising for others.

'Different metaphors may be more or less appropriate for different people or for the same person at different times.'

The seven-strong project team is looking at metaphors in a 1.5-million collection of words consisting of personal interviews and contributions to online forums. The researchers will analyse and interpret each metaphor used, the context in which it is used, the implications for the individual's experience, and differences within and across the three groups.

Combining qualitative and quantitative research methods, the project will exploit an innovative semantic annotation tool, embedded in a web-based system called 'Wmatrix', developed by project team member Dr Paul Rayson, a Senior Lecturer at Lancaster University's School of Computing and Communications.

Health psychologist and expert in end-of-life studies Professor Sheila Payne, a member of the project team, is keen for the study to be used to inform policy making and the training of health professionals.

She explained: 'By analysing the language people use, we should be able to come up with conclusions that improve communication between the three groups involved in end-of-life care. A better understanding of people's uses of metaphor can help to identify possible sources of misunderstanding.'

The work is attracting significant interest from academics and health professionals in Europe and China who want to replicate the project in their countries.

An end-of-project event will take place in May 2014 at The Work Foundation in London when government officials involved in cancer and end-of-life care strategy, senior NHS officials and policymakers will be invited to hear and respond to the project findings. There will also be places for senior academics involved in health research and for health practitioners involved in end-of-life care.

There will also be a web-based seminar at Lancaster University's International Observatory on End of Life Care in April 2014.

## More

For more information, visit the project website: ucrel.lancs.ac.uk/melc/index.php

*Dying Matters is not responsible for the content of external websites.*

*1 October 2013*

⇨ The above information is reprinted with kind permission from Dying Matters. Please visit www.dyingmatters.org for further information.

© Dying Matters 2014

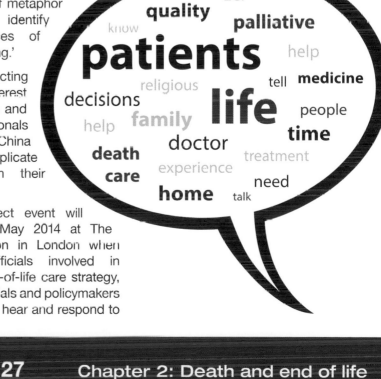

# Your legal rights and responsibilities

*A Good Funeral Guide factsheet.*

## Who's in charge?

There's no law that says you have to have a funeral.

But there is a law that says you must dispose of the body of the person who has died 'by burial, cremation or any other means' (Births and Deaths Registration Act 1953).

The law views a dead body as a potential health hazard and it enables one or more people to take possession of a dead body for the sole purpose of disposing of it. Note that word 'possession'. Possessing a dead body is not the same as owning it. No one owns a dead body. No one owns a living body, either. You do not own your own body; you are not allowed to offer your organs for sale.

Certain people have a prior right to possess a dead body so long as they undertake to dispose of it. If you have the right to take possession of a dead body then you have the right do so at once without having to produce any documentation.

## What does this mean?

The person with the right to possess the body has the right to take possession as soon as death happens – there's no need to pick up a death certificate on the way, you can get that later. The only person with a prior right to take possession of the body is the coroner.

If someone dies at home you can keep them there. If someone dies in a hospital or a hospice you can bring them home. Don't let anyone tell you otherwise.

You don't have to hide the body from view but you must not expose it naked in public or in such a way as to 'outrage public decency'.

If you want to care for someone who has died at home you'll need to be able, at the very least, to keep them cool.

Dead bodies pose no risk of infection if a) the person did not die of a notifiable disease or b) is not leaking any blood. Infectious agents thrive in living bodies, not dead ones.

You may be told, even by people in authority who ought to know better, that, when someone dies, you must engage a funeral director. WRONG. You are in charge: the person who has died is your responsibility. It is entirely up to you to decide whether or not you want to pay someone else – an undertaker – to look after your dead person for you.

## Who has to right to take possession of the body?

There are two categories of people who have no automatic right either to possess the body with the intention of disposing of it or to inherit from the estate.

The first of these is next of kin. The term next of kin is legally meaningless. The person who has died may have nominated someone as his or her next of kin, but that gives them no right to dispose of the body unless named as an executor, and no right to inherit unless named in the will.

The second is an unmarried partner, or one who is not legally registered as being in a civil partnership with the person who has died. Such a partner has no right to dispose of the body unless named as an executor and no right to inherit unless named in the will. This is the cruellest consequence of failing to make a will.

## What legally has to be done?

Your legal duty is limited to satisfying the state that:

⇨ cause of death has been certified and recorded for the detection of foul play and the reporting of accurate health and disease information.

⇨ the body was buried, cremated, or otherwise satisfactorily disposed of within a reasonable period.

The death must be certified by a doctor who has provided care during the last illness and who has seen the person who died within 14 days of death (28 days in Northern Ireland) or after death. (There is no legal definition of death in the UK.)

The death must be reported by a qualified person to the registrar within five days.

The registrar will issue:

⇨ a Certificate for Burial and Cremation, also known as the green form, giving the go-ahead for the person's body to be buried or for you to apply for cremation.

⇨ a Certificate of Registration of Death (form BD8, also known as a death certificate) for use in dealing with the dead person's state pension or other benefits.

If you want to bury the person who has died you can now go ahead.

## Cremation

If you want to cremate the person who has died there's more to do. You must

⇨ apply for cremation by filling in the form.

⇨ ensure that a second doctor certifies cause of death.

The reason why a second doctor must certify the death is to avoid a situation where a) doubt is later expressed concerning cause of death or b) it is suspected the person has surely been murdered by their doctor (e.g. Dr Shipman) or somebody else. If a body is buried it can be dug up (exhumed) and tested. If it's been cremated it can't.

When you apply for cremation, the doctor who first certified the death plus the second doctor must support your application. These forms – the application for cremation plus certification of cause of death by both doctors – are examined by the medical referee at the crematorium. When the referee is satisfied, they fill in a form.

If you want to inspect the medical certificates submitted by the two doctors (Forms Cremation 4 and Cremation 5) before the medical referee authorises the cremation you can do that.

## If there's a will there's an executor

If the person who has died made a will and named an executor, then the executor, whether a family member or not, has the right to possess the body, register the death and make disposal arrangements, together with the option of arranging a funeral.

Often a person will name more than one executor. They are all equal. They are joint possessors of the body. If a local solicitor is one of the executors or even the sole executor he or she is unlikely to meddle unless those arranging the funeral propose to spend an unreasonable amount of money in relation to the size of the estate.

## Where there's no will there's an administrator

If the person who has died did not make a will (has died intestate), what then? The answer is that a court of law will appoint the closest living relative to be the administrator of the estate, with inheritance rights and, also, the right to possess the body, register the death and make disposal arrangements, together with the option to arrange a funeral. If there is more than one administrator they are all equal.

## When executors and administrators can't agree

When family members have strong and differing views and beliefs, they may find it difficult to agree about funeral arrangements (among other things). Although executors and administrators are urged by the law to take each other's feelings into account, this is wishful thinking unenforceable in law.

If you are in this position it is vital that you reach agreement on important matters before one of you registers the death. Each will probably have to give ground over some issues so that each can have their way in others. Where victory is impossible, compromise is essential.

If you opt for cremation, there is an application form that will ask you: is there any near relative(s) or executor(s) who has not been informed of the proposed cremation? This is to prevent someone from cremating the body without your knowledge, and to prevent you from cremating it without your fellow executors' or administrators' knowledge. It also covers a circumstance where an executor refuses to arrange disposal and someone else undertakes to do so instead.

The form will also ask you: has any near relative or executor expressed any objection to the proposed cremation? In such a circumstance, the objector can seek an injunction in a court of law to prevent the cremation.

## Do you have to accept responsibility?

No one has to accept responsibility for disposing of someone who has died. There is no legal penalty if you refuse, but you won't be able to hold a funeral. If everyone else refuses as well, the dead person's local authority, or the hospital in which they died, has a legal duty to dispose of the body under the Public Health (Control of Disease) Act 1984 (and it will almost certainly hold a funeral, too). It will retrieve the expense from the dead person's estate if there are sufficient assets.

If you really can't afford to hold a funeral, this is a real option for you – far better than falling into the jaws of loan sharks. You will be allowed to attend the funeral and no one will chase you for money afterwards.

## Does it matter what the person who died wanted?

No. The possessor of the body can dispose of it as he or she wishes, no matter what the dead person stipulated when alive. Disposal and funeral wishes have no legal standing whatever.

## Alternatives to immediate disposal

There are three alternatives to immediate disposal, none of which is available to you unless the dead person made provision when they were alive. If the person who has died opted for one of these, you will know all about it. These alternatives are:

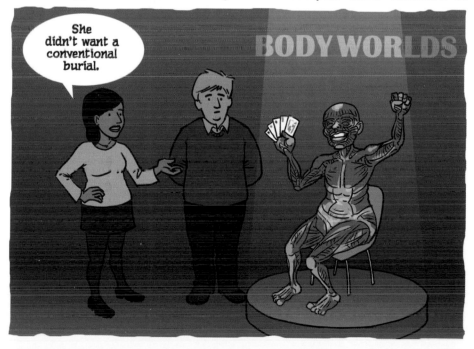

- ⇨ Donation of the body to medical science to be dissected by students. This will delay disposal by up to five years

- ⇨ Cryonic preservation: keeping the body frozen in liquid nitrogen until medical science can find a way of reviving it

- ⇨ Plastination: a process whereby water is drawn out of the body and replaced by polymers which set hard, after which it is posed and displayed in a Bodyworlds exhibition.

**Disposal is compulsory and legally enforceable.**

## The funeral

Official guidance often uses the term 'funeral arrangements' wrongly to mean disposal arrangements. It may seem kinder to talk about a funeral rather than disposal but it is also, in this respect, misleading. Though we normally think of a funeral as an event comprising a ceremony together with either cremation or burial, the law doesn't. The law concerns itself exclusively with disposal.

A funeral is a farewell ceremony or event at which a dead body is present before it is buried or cremated. A funeral fulfills an emotional and sometimes also a spiritual need. There are no laws governing funerals

Anyone can lead a funeral – there's no official qualification for the job. You can do anything you like at a funeral so long as it is within the law – and the regulations of the venue.

## Who pays?

The person who, at the registrar's office, signs the death certificate will be given a certificate for burial or cremation (the green form) and will be held responsible for making it happen. A registrar will be reluctant to proceed with registration if it is evident that the executors are wrangling.

The person who makes arrangements with a funeral director makes him or herself responsible for paying the bill. A funeral director will be reluctant to enter into a contract if he or she is aware of family disagreements. Having entered into a contract, the funeral director will answer directly to the contractee and no one else.

**A funeral is an option, not a legal necessity.**

- ⇨ The above information is reprinted with kind permission from Good Funeral Guide. Please visit www.goodfuneralguide.co.uk for further information.

# Wills and probate

## *Securing the future: less than half have a will.*

### By Ben Tomin

Fewer than half (41%) of all adults say that they currently have a will. However, that number does rise significantly after the age of 55; almost three quarters of that group do have one (71%). Only two in five (42%) of 45- to 54-year-olds have a will.

For those who haven't made a will, over half (53%) say they have not got round to it, while 11% say they know they need to, and that they will get round to it. This shows an area where companies can attract new clients. A significant majority (68%), say that they are too young to make a will, and 20% say they have no assets to pass on.

A change in health is a prompt to make a will for 38% of respondents. Financial reasons are the motivation for 23%. Over half say getting married (52%) and having children (52%) are the key motivators. The loss of a loved one leads to a decision for 27%. Separation (62%) is the main reason a person would choose to change the contents of their will.

Over half (55%) say the reason they make a will, regardless of what has prompted them to, is to ensure their estate is distributed in the way they intend. Half (50%) say it is to secure the future of their family.

The will-writing market in Britain has an estimated value of between £700 million and £900 million. Figures from the probate service show that almost 250,000 families go through probate court every year. 63% of those with a will say they used a law firm of solicitors, compared with 12% who completed the will entirely themselves.

While 52% believe that law firms and solicitors are the best qualified to prepare a will, the same percentage would be willing to try and prepare an online will themselves if it meant the costs could be kept down.

In May 2013, the Lord Chancellor decided not to regulate the will-writing market. When consumers are asked about the decision, half say they have concerns that it will make it difficult for them to choose a quality provider over a poor one. 39% do agree that it will bring more consumer choice into the market.

Inheritance tax is due when the value of a person's estate reaches £325,000 or more. Consumer knowledge regarding the specifics of this tax is patchy at best. 28% know exactly what the threshold is, while a quarter (25%) have no idea, and 315 say the threshold is at too low a level. 20% know the rate of tax is 40% but 41% do not know.

Knowledge about the 'Rules of Intestacy' (when there is no will or a void will) is lower still. One in ten (10%) of adults know what they are and how they work. Over a third (34%) have never heard of them.

*20 January 2014*

- ⇨ The above information is reprinted with kind permission from YouGov. Please visit www.yougov.co.uk for further information.

# Attending a funeral

Attending a funeral is always a difficult time. If you are attending a funeral for the first time, there may be many questions that you have about funeral etiquette – what happens at a funeral, what to wear, even whether you should attend.

We hope the following information will help to answer some of your questions. Funeral customs and traditions do differ, so our information can only be a guide - if you need more detailed information, the Funeral Director or Celebrant will be in a position to help.

## Deciding whether to go to a funeral

### Should I attend a funeral?

If you are trying to decide whether or not to go to a funeral then the answer is probably yes – go if you can. You do not need to be invited; a funeral service is open to anyone, unless the family ask specifically that it is a private ceremony. Those arranging the funeral will appreciate you being there.

### Taking children

This is entirely a personal decision and it is perfectly acceptable to take children to a funeral, but toddlers and babies can be bored and/or disruptive, especially if it's a long service. If they start to make a lot of noise, parents generally take them outside during the ceremony itself.

With older children you could ask them if they want to go and if they do then it's a good idea to explain it fully beforehand so they know what to expect.

## What to wear to a funeral

People attending a funeral don't dress entirely in black these days, most people choose to wear more formal clothes like a suit, dress or jacket.

Men generally remove their hats during the actual service and often wear a black or dark tie. The main thing is not to wear clothes that would draw attention to you by being too casual, flamboyant or revealing.

Some people think that bright clothing is not appropriate but others may ask everyone to wear a particularly bright colour or type of clothing. It is worth checking beforehand with those organising the funeral.

It is worth noting that some religions have specific clothing requirements – for example at Greek Orthodox ceremonies you are expected to cover your head. You can call the funeral director arranging the funeral for the family for advice on this.

If there is to be a burial, you will be outside for at least some of the funeral so make sure you have warm clothing. It could be muddy and slippery, so wear flat rather than high-heeled shoes or boots. Churches and some crematoria can be also quite cold in winter months. The most important thing is to be comfortable and dress for the weather. Don't forget an umbrella if the weather merits it.

## Getting to the funeral

### The day of the funeral, take with you:

⇨ Mobile phone – with a mental note to turn it off before the funeral starts

⇨ Details of the location

⇨ Money in case of donations

⇨ Change for car park

⇨ Mobile phone numbers of other people who will be attending

⇨ Flowers if they haven't been sent in advance

⇨ Words you are going to say if you are taking part

⇨ Tissues

### Getting there

Plan to arrive early! Leave at least half an hour extra in case of delays. Allow additional time for parking and then walking to the location.

Plan your journey carefully including any stops. Many people get lost finding cemeteries and crematoria, which is understandable as they can be in remote, unfamiliar locations. Look up the postcode of the location on funeralmap.co.uk and use a sat nav if you can. Otherwise download a journey plan from AA Route Planner, freely available on www.theaa.com.

Find out in advance if there is car parking or a nearby car park and what the cost will be.

Find out if there are any refreshments and toilet facilities at the location or nearby. If you arrive early do NOT go to the house where the funeral procession will be leaving from unless you have been asked to be a part of the procession. The family will not be pleased to see unexpected visitors at this time.

Most churches and crematoria do have toilet facilities, although most do not have refreshments available. Cemeteries tend to have no facilities at all, although natural burial sites may have toilet facilities and/or refreshments.

### If you are going to be late

Call someone else attending the funeral so they can tell the family you are delayed and roughly how long you expect to be. There is nothing worse than close family being aware that you have not arrived and trying to delay the funeral to wait for you.

### Car parking

Crematoria – car parking is usually available but find out beforehand where parking is located or where local car parks are situated. Have enough change for the car park with you. Public transport is usually available to crematoria but you need to check timetables.

Cemeteries – many cemeteries do not have a car park so on-street parking will be needed, or use a nearby car park. If you are taking anyone to the funeral that cannot walk very far, then consider dropping them off at the nearest point and then parking the car.

Churches – some churches have small car parks but many do not, so the same applies as regards parking and dropping off anyone who needs closer access.

Natural Burial Parks – as the majority of these sites have been created in the last 20 years, ample car parking is usually available.

At all funeral locations, don't park on grassed areas unless directed to do so.

### Multiple venues

Sometimes funerals involve more than one location, which can't be walked to. For example, the ceremony or service might be held in a church and be followed by a burial in a churchyard or cemetery, which may not be near the church.

If the funeral involves different locations and you are travelling by public transport, ask the family if anyone attending will be able to give you a lift to the second location.

If you are driving then you will go to your car after the ceremony and, along with all the other mourners, you will drive to the grave location. Make sure you know in advance where the location is as you can easily get separated from someone you are following.

## The funeral procession

The person arranging the funeral decides who will be in the cars or limousines following the hearse – this is usually family members and sometimes close friends. Most of the people going to the funeral will use their own cars and may choose to meet the procession where the service is being held.

Usually the funeral procession leaves from the home of the person who has died.

Unless you have been invited to participate in the funeral procession, it is not advisable to turn up at the house from where the funeral procession will be leaving – the family will not be pleased to see unexpected visitors at this time.

## The funeral ceremony

### Entering the church, chapel or crematorium

In some cases you will be ushered in to take your seat before the family and coffin arrive; at other funerals, you might wait until they have arrived and you walk in behind them.

The front rows are for the immediate family so sit nearer the back if you did not know the person very well. However, if there are few mourners present then sit nearer to the front. It does not matter which side of the 'aisle' you sit.

### If you are asked to carry the coffin

If you are asked by the family to carry the coffin then accept and be honoured to have been asked. The funeral director will make sure that you are clearly instructed in what you need to do.

You will usually carry the coffin to the front of the church or crematorium. In the case of a burial you will again carry to the hearse and then to the grave, or directly to the grave if it is close by.

### What to expect during the funeral ceremony

In a church or other religious building, the ceremony will be conducted by a minister of religion. In a crematorium or at a natural burial site, the ceremony may be led by a funeral celebrant or humanist officiant.

At most funerals there is likely to be an 'Order of Ceremony' provided when you arrive. This is yours to keep and it will help you see what will happen during the ceremony. It will detail any hymns or songs, who will speak and the order in which everything will happen. It may also state where the family would like you to go for refreshments afterwards, and what to do with any donations you may wish to make.

During the ceremony you might be asked to sit or stand, pray, sing or listen to music. You might be asked to release a balloon, write a message or place a flower on the coffin. You might be given some seeds or bulbs to plant in memory of the person. These days there is so much choice in funeral ceremonies that everyone is different and there are limitless ways that families can influence what happens at the funeral.

In a crematorium chapel, the coffin may remain on view, become hidden by a curtain (or a transparent curtain may remain in place) or it may be lowered into the floor.

### Showing emotion

People cry at funerals – everyone understands this, and also that some people don't cry. Everyone grieves differently and shows different levels of emotion. There is no right or wrong here, it's about showing your support. Just being there shows that you care. Have tissues with you and keep make-up to a minimum if you think you will be very upset.

## Leaving at the end of the funeral

### At a crematorium

At the end of the ceremony the person conducting it will make it clear that the ceremony has finished. The chief mourners leave first, followed by everyone else. You will wait until the rows in front of you leave and you file out after them. You might walk past the coffin (it will not be open as this is not the practice in the UK) and you might want to just stop for a moment or touch the coffin lightly as you leave.

Everyone files out and stands around the flower terrace, which is an opportunity to speak to the family and other mourners before leaving to go to the wake or gathering afterwards.

In the case of a ceremony held in a hall or other venue, close family might be attending the cremation afterwards on their own, so everyone will gather outside as the coffin is placed in the hearse.

### At a burial

If the grave is nearby, everyone will drive or walk from the chapel to the graveside behind the coffin and further words will be spoken before the coffin is lowered into the grave.

If chairs have been placed at a graveside, they are for those who are infirm or for the immediate family members; others will be expected to stand.

Avoid walking directly on graves if you can and stay between the headstones.

At many burials, earth or other items such as flowers or rose petals are thrown into the grave at the end of the service. Sometimes only immediate family does this and sometimes all the mourners follow and do this as well. Watch others and if you feel it appropriate to do so, there is no reason for you not to follow suit.

⇨ The above information is reprinted with kind permission from Funeralmap. Please visit www.funeralmap.co.uk for further information.

# Reflecting personality prevalent in a modern-day funeral

**A new YouGov report shows that funeral planning in the UK is becoming increasingly personalised and tailored to the individual involved, as more and more people consider the service they would like after death.**

**By Ben Tobin**

Two thirds (66%) of UK adults have had some thoughts about the kind of funeral ceremony they would like. This rises to nearly three quarters (73%) for those aged 55+. An even larger percentage have thought about whether they would like to be buried or cremated, with 91% of the same age group having given this dilemma some consideration.

Women are more likely than men to have started to think about their own funeral service. In the 40–54 age group, 55% of men have thought about their funeral plans, as compared to 70% of women. This is important for marketers to recognise, as women may also be able to persuade men to think about their own plans.

The modern nature of funeral services is underlined in one instance by the use of music. Increasingly, songs such as My Way (Frank Sinatra) and Monty Python's Always Look on the Bright Side of Life, are being chosen over traditional, sombre church music to reflect the personality of the deceased. Six in ten (58%) chose to have recorded music at a ceremony, with just a third (33%) opting for a musician such as an organist.

Almost all (96%) those who organised a funeral in the past five years used a funeral director; however, 44% chose one that they were already familiar with, indicating how vital it is for funeral directors to build strong trusting relationships with families as they may well be called upon again in the future.

James McCoy, Research Director at YouGov said, 'The study shows that families and friends are often looking to move away from an overly morose and sombre atmosphere at funerals, by reflecting the deceased's personality and interests in the ceremony.

Of course, funeral planning occurs at an upsetting and stressful time; it is therefore important for funeral directors to continue to forge relationships with families and friends in order to establish ways in which the specific wishes of the deceased and family can be honoured and translated into the service.'

*21 March 2014*

⇨ The above information is reprinted with kind permission from YouGov. Please visit www.yougov.co.uk for further information.

# How to afford a funeral

*By Justin Schamotta*

According to the University of Bath's Institute for Policy Research, the average cost of funeral and burial or cremation is now around £3,500.

This is a 7.1% rise since last year, and a massive 80% rise since 2004. The International Longevity Centre UK predicts that costs will continue their dramatic increase for at least the next five years.

However, there are ways to save.

This guide provides information on the costs to be aware of when planning a funeral, and what help is available to meet any monetary shortfalls.

## Funeral costs: what to pay

Unlike other consumer choices, arranging and paying for a funeral doesn't typically involve shopping around for the best price.

According to a Sun Life Direct *Cost of Dying* report, fewer than 10% of consumers go to more than one funeral director when planning a funeral.

Just as elsewhere, however, it pays to be aware of what costs are involved beforehand and how comparing services can bring costs down.

### Funeral directors

Most people contact funeral directors to carry out the administrative work in arranging a funeral.

Those who operate under a code of practice and have an established complaints procedure will be registered either with the National Association of Funeral Directors or the Society of Allied and Independent Funeral Directors.

Alternatively, arranging a DIY funeral can make you significant savings, but is likely of course to add significant amounts of stress at an already stressful time.

### Cremation or burial?

The average cost of cremation has risen by 4.7%, while the average cost of burial has risen by 5.7%. Figures from Mintel suggest that burial typically costs around £1,000 more than a cremation.

Cremation costs can be further reduced with the option of a direct cremation. This no-frills service involves the company collecting the body, cremating it, and then returning the ashes. Direct cremation costs around £1,000.

It's worth bearing in mind that burial fees will increase with the introduction of death certification fees later on in 2014. At the moment, death certificates are provided by doctors and are only necessary for cremations.

### Memorials

Memorial stones are one of the most expensive components of a funeral, costing anything from £200 to several thousand pounds. On average, say Mintel, people pay £864.

An alternative is to create an online memorial website instead.

This can link to a charity organisation supported by the deceased, and offers a far cheaper alternative.

### Coffins

Though a flat packed cardboard coffin from China can be bought for as little as £15, most people opt for something a little more upmarket.

Most coffins range in price from between £300 and £1,000. Websites such as comparethecoffin.com can help cut costs and have more information on the many types of coffin available, from traditional wood and metal to cardboard or fabric.

### Transport

Funeral directors typically arrange the transportation of the body to the funeral. However, UK law doesn't restrict the movement of dead bodies by the next of kin (unless they cross the Scottish border).

If you would like to arrange the transportation of the body to the funeral, then you are within your rights to do so.

### Flowers

80% of those tasked with arranging a funeral buy flowers, and spend an average of £160. Opting for homemade arrangements can personalise the experience and reduce overall costs.

## Getting help: funeral payments

Unfortunately, there's very little help available to the more than 100,000 people that struggle to pay for a funeral every year.

The assistance that is available has been deemed woefully inadequate by policy-making organisations and consumer groups such as Citizen's Advice.

However, it's still worth checking whether you might be entitled to help with costs.

### Social Fund Funeral Payment

The main help offered by the Government is via the Social Fund Funeral Payment (FP) scheme, which is overseen by the Department for Work and Pensions (DWP).

Between 2012 and 2013, the average award for successful applicants was £1,225, which is approximately a third of the average cost of a funeral and burial or cremation.

The recipient of the FP grant may have to pay it back if they subsequently receive any money from the deceased person's estate.

### Who's eligible?

Around 40,000 benefit-dependent families a year are awarded with a FP grant. On average, just over 54% of claims are successful.

Eligible candidates must be either: the parent of the deceased, the partner, a close relative or a close friend.

Candidates must also be claiming one of the following benefits:

⇨ Income Support or income-based Jobseeker's Allowance

⇨ Income-related Employment and Support Allowance

⇨ Pension Credit

⇨ Housing Benefit

⇨ The disability or severe disability element of Working Tax Credit

⇨ One of the extra elements of Child Tax Credit

⇨ Universal Credit.

### How to apply

Applications must be made within three months of the funeral by calling the Bereavement Service helpline on 0845 606 0265, or by visiting the Government site.

Somewhat perversely, claimants must arrange the funeral before they can apply to the FP scheme.

They must provide an invoice for the funeral with the claim, before the DWP decides how much, if anything, they will receive.

This approach has understandably been criticised – most recently in a report compiled by researchers at the University of Bath.

### Public Health Funerals

Those who have been refused help from the FP scheme, and who cannot afford to meet funeral costs any other way may be forced to opt for a Public Health Funeral.

These are administered by local authorities, which have a duty under public health law to dispose of bodies that no one is otherwise taking responsibility for.

Public Health Funerals involve a simple service for the deceased, after which they are either cremated

or buried in an unmarked communal grave. Though traditionally known as a pauper's funeral, the stigma attached to Public Health Funerals is seemingly waning.

A report from the Local Government Association estimated that there are around 2,900 such funerals a year.

*28 February 2014*

⇨ The above information is reprinted with kind permission from Choose. Please visit www.choose.net for further information.

*© 2003-2014 Choose Ltd*

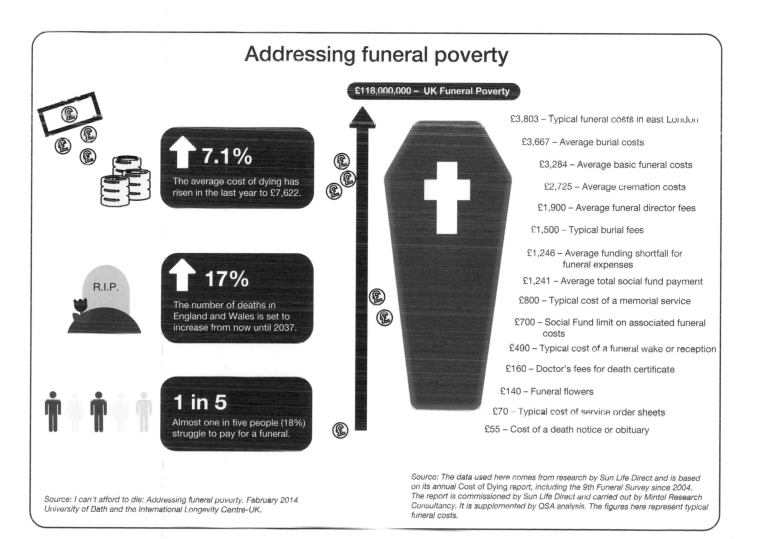

# Addressing funeral poverty

**£118,000,000 – UK Funeral Poverty**

↑ **7.1%**
The average cost of dying has risen in the last year to £7,622.

↑ **17%**
The number of deaths in England and Wales is set to increase from now until 2037.

R.I.P.

**1 in 5**
Almost one in five people (18%) struggle to pay for a funeral.

£3,803 – Typical funeral costs in east London

£3,667 – Average burial costs

£3,284 – Average basic funeral costs

£2,725 – Average cremation costs

£1,900 – Average funeral director fees

£1,500 – Typical burial fees

£1,246 – Average funding shortfall for funeral expenses

£1,241 – Average total social fund payment

£800 – Typical cost of a memorial service

£700 – Social Fund limit on associated funeral costs

£490 – Typical cost of a funeral wake or reception

£160 – Doctor's fees for death certificate

£140 – Funeral flowers

£70 – Typical cost of service order sheets

£55 – Cost of a death notice or obituary

Source: I can't afford to die: Addressing funeral poverty. February 2014. University of Bath and the International Longevity Centre-UK.

Source: The data used here comes from research by Sun Life Direct and is based on its annual Cost of Dying report, including the 9th Funeral Survey since 2004. The report is commissioned by Sun Life Direct and carried out by Mintel Research Consultancy. It is supplemented by QSA analysis. The figures here represent typical funeral costs.

# The green funeral revolution

*Jackie Macadam learns more about environmental funerals and how new options are being offered in death.*

'She sat in the front pew every week with her family and everyone knew her. Her death was sudden and unexpected, and when she died, everyone responded with baking and love.

'Her family wanted her funeral to be pared down with no fuss. They wanted it to include the many voices of those who loved her, and not just the minister, telling her story.

'She'd been one of the original flower people, wasting nothing, renovating and recycling as much as possible, and in death, it was wholly appropriate that things would be the same.

'She'd already planned most of her own funeral, ordering a beautiful wicker casket, specified only wild flowers in season, or living flowers. She died in January. The casket was filled with bunches of dried lavender and the top was decorated with them too – the scent hung in the air in the church, and somehow it reminded us of her as well. The church entrance was filled with daffodils and crocuses – hinting at the Spring to come.

'The service was simple, but loving. Her favourite hymn, a poem she had chosen, a letter from her grandchildren and that was it. She was buried in the church graveyard. We had thought about going to the eco-burial site, but it was seven miles away, and this had been her home.'

The Rev. Julie Woods recalls the experience she had of a different sort of funeral she took part in at her parish in Earlston.

'It was an entirely appropriate send-off to a woman who loved nature and the natural world,' she says.

Funerals are changing and ministers find themselves finding that they need to change with them. People are planning their funerals in ways that could not have been imagined in the past. Coffins now come in wicker, cardboard and even heavy felt; some people are opting for a full 'eco' funeral, buried in one of the eco sites springing up around the country and trying to minimise their environmental impact as much as possible.

Jamie Pearson is an independent funeral director based in Glasgow and a recommended funeral director by the Natural Death Centre.

'Eco tends to mean different things to different people,' he says. 'For most it ends with a woodland burial which can allow for a greater choice than a conventional funeral in style of coffin and service.

'For woodland funerals, the coffins must be biodegradable, for instance using cardboard or willow; there can be no embalming or toxic chemicals used on the body or the coffin, and often a tree is planted in place of a headstone.'

> **'The service was simple, but loving. Her favourite hymn, a poem she had chosen, a letter from her grandchildren and that was it. She was buried in the church graveyard. We had thought about going to the eco-burial site, but it was seven miles away, and this had been her home'**

Sarah Gray is a director of Binning Memorial Wood in East Lothian. It's an established woodland, covering around 300 acres.

'Being an established woodland, we don't plant a tree above the person. We work with the trees and the natural woodland when we bury people, trying to find spaces that cause as little disruption to the trees as possible. Graves are marked with a wooden or bronze plaque if the family wants, and we use a digital marker so that we know exactly where everyone is interred.'

Like everything else in life, we are putting more thought into planning for our own deaths; choosing to do things with more thought to the land and the environment and sometimes turning away from the traditional churchyard burial.

As churchyards fill up, our ministers are getting involved in this new embracing of the green revolution and ensuring that the church still has a place, in the future as well as the present.

*This is an abridged version of a feature in June's* Life and Work.

*27 May 2014*

⇨ This article appeared in the June 2014 issue of *Life and Work*, the editorially independent magazine of the Church of Scotland. www.lifeandwork.org.

# Your digital legacy – what happens to your online data after you die?

**When we think of the sentimental legacies we'll leave our children, no longer will it be boxes of family photographs, handwritten diaries and our much-loved CD collection.**

With over 21 million UK households now having Internet access and 67% of us 'logging on' each day we are increasingly living our lives online.

Our photograph albums, diaries and CDs have been replaced with online photo-sharing websites, social media sites and music accounts either stored on a device or on a 'cloud'.

However, our new digital lives could present a problem after we die. How do we pass these online items of our family history to the next generation and how are our online financial arrangements to be dealt with on death?

With new media presenting new difficulties for executors tasked with administering a person's estate on death, it is becoming increasingly important that we consider the extent of our online life – both financial and sentimental – and include these digital assets in our overall estate plan.

We've asked Aileen Entwistle, an associate at Anderson Strathern Solicitors to explain what needs to be done to protect our digital legacy for future generations.

## Financial arrangements

Whether it be everyday banking, savings accounts, online investment portfolios and share-trading accounts, online shopping or betting and gaming accounts, many of us have an online financial presence in one form or another. It is important to keep an up-to-date record of online accounts otherwise you run the risk of these potentially valuable accounts being overlooked when your estate is being wound up. But be careful – don't leave a note of your PIN number or passwords as this is likely to breach the bank's conditions. An executor accessing an online account using the deceased's username and password could also be committing a criminal offence of 'unauthorised access' under the Computer Misuse Act 1990. It will be enough to simply leave a note of the bank and account number. An informal writing is preferable to leaving a legacy of specific accounts (or password details) in your will as you can then keep your records current without having to continuously update your will.

The process of dealing with online accounts after death is relatively simple. Financial institutions will typically require sight of a death certificate plus confirmation from court (depending upon the account's value) to release information and funds. For eBay or PayPal accounts, they will require a death certificate and confirmation plus the executor's ID before it will pay out funds. eBay will close an account or eBay shop, it will not transfer ownership and failure to complete an agreed transaction due to death could result in a legal liability on the estate.

For those operating a website for personal or business purposes, it is important to take legal advice in relation to the registration of the domain names and other associated intellectual property. This will help to ensure the website can continue to operate and be maintained by the business or be left to the chosen beneficiary.

He requested a picture for his final facebook status update.

click!

## E-mail and social media

Each digital service provider has a different procedure for closing a deceased's account. They will request proof of death (death certificate and sometimes a link to a published obituary) as well as confirmation of the executor or family member's relationship to the deceased user.

Facebook gives families two options: delete the profile or set up a memorial page. If memorialised, the user's personal information will be removed, and no one can log on to the account, but the user's wall will remain and existing friends and family can leave messages.

Twitter will close the account and help families to recover an archive of the user's public tweets. In contrast, e-mail providers are generally quite clear that they will honour the user's privacy and not release any record of e-mail exchanges without a court order.

## Photos

Flickr had six billion images stored on it in 2011. It has a limited free service but requires a regular subscription to access all photos held on an account. If the account is inactive for 90 days, Flickr may close the account. Arrangements must be made for executors to keep paying for the subscription if they wish to keep the photographs. The simplest answer for photos is to keep a back-up on memory card or CD.

## iTunes, Kindle

We don't actually own the music in our iTunes accounts and our Kindle book collection, we only have a lifetime licence. The small print specifies that these rights terminate on death and are not transferable, even if we access our collection on a PC, device or Kindle which is owned or used by another family member. This could come as a shock to a user who has spent a considerable amount of money building up their music or book collection. If we want to pass on such items then we'll need to start buying the tangible versions again.

Digital asset planning will only increase in importance as we continue to upload more of our life online. The law needs to catch up but, until then, plan your digital afterlife by keeping a running inventory of our accounts and passwords (including device passwords), ensuring it's kept in a safe place. Back up your photographs and take legal advice if you have particularly valuable online assets. It's also good planning to review your will and grant a power of attorney as the problems surrounding access to your digital life aren't confined to death but will also apply if you lose capacity. And finally, let your family know of the digital asset planning you have undertaken so that these valuable or sentimental assets aren't ignored when you log off for good.

*11 June 2013*

⇨ The above information is reprinted with kind permission from *The Herald*. Please visit www.heraldscotland.com for further information.

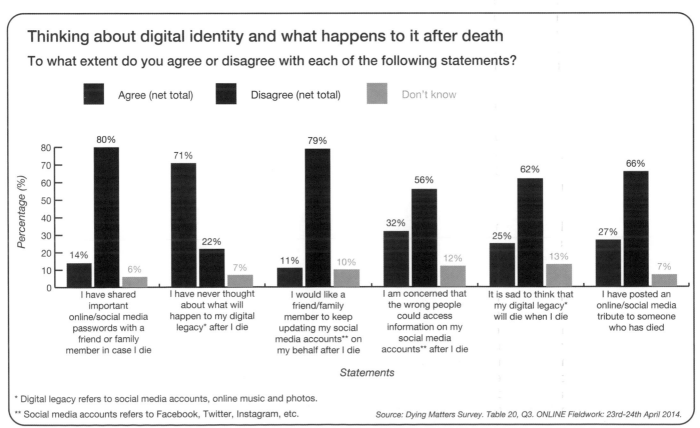

### Thinking about digital identity and what happens to it after death

To what extent do you agree or disagree with each of the following statements?

Legend: ■ Agree (net total)  ■ Disagree (net total)  ■ Don't know

| Statement | Agree | Disagree | Don't know |
|---|---|---|---|
| I have shared important online/social media passwords with a friend or family member in case I die | 14% | 80% | 6% |
| I have never thought about what will happen to my digital legacy* after I die | 71% | 22% | 7% |
| I would like a friend/family member to keep updating my social media accounts** on my behalf after I die | 11% | 79% | 10% |
| I am concerned that the wrong people could access information on my social media accounts** after I die | 32% | 56% | 12% |
| It is sad to think that my digital legacy* will die when I die | 25% | 62% | 13% |
| I have posted an online/social media tribute to someone who has died | 27% | 66% | 7% |

*Statements*

\* Digital legacy refers to social media accounts, online music and photos.
\*\* Social media accounts refers to Facebook, Twitter, Instagram, etc.

*Source: Dying Matters Survey. Table 20, Q3. ONLINE Fieldwork: 23rd-24th April 2014.*

# First opt-out organ donation scheme in UK set to be approved in Wales

## Under new bill, adults would be assumed to have consented to use of organs and tissues unless they stipulate otherwise.

*By Steve Morris*

The first organ donation scheme in the UK that puts the onus on citizens to opt out if they do not wish to take part is set to be given the go-ahead on Tuesday.

Welsh Assembly members are to vote on a controversial bill under which adults will be deemed to have consented to their organs and tissue being used if they have not stipulated otherwise.

The Welsh Government believes the law will increase the number of organs available, save dozens of lives every year and, if successful, could be copied in other parts of the UK.

Opponents claim the move gives the state too much control over people's bodies, could cause extra distress for bereaved families and puts medical staff in a difficult position.

Concerns have been raised that the infrastructure may not be in place to make use of more organs and some even suggest that adverse publicity about the scheme could lead to a backlash and a drop in the number available.

Under the so-called 'soft opt-out system', adults who live and die in Wales will be able to register a wish to be a donor or opt out. If they have done neither they will be deemed to have given their consent.

Families will not have a veto in law, but they will be given the chance to show that the deceased person would not have wished to donate their organs.

Mark Drakeford, the Welsh Health Minister, said: 'We have the enduring problem of not having enough organs for people who need them. About one person every week dies in Wales while on a waiting list. We have been working to improve the rate of organ donation and have had some success, but we're looking to take the next step forward.

'Around a third of the Welsh population is on the organ donor register, but well over two-thirds in surveys say they are happy to be organ donors. That other third is people who don't get round to putting their names down. We're hoping to make inroads into that.'

Drakeford said if the bill was passed it would be the most significant law since the assembly was given full law-making powers two years ago and, if it worked, there could be a 'domino effect' in other parts of the UK.

He accepted the role of families in the process was controversial and that some faith groups had problems with the scheme. Members of the Muslim Council of Wales and the South Wales Jewish Representative Council have expressed reservations. 'We know people from minority ethnic communities need donors more often and yet their levels of donation are amongst the lowest,' Drakeford said. 'We're very keen to work actively with them to allay any fears.'

Barry Morgan, the Archbishop of Wales, led criticism of the Human Transplantation (Wales) bill, telling *The Guardian* that giving organs was a 'great act of love', but that he opposed the system that is expected to become law. 'Donation ought to be a gift of love, of generosity. If organs can be taken unless someone has explicitly registered an objection, that's not an expression of love. It's more a medical use of a body,' he said.

Surgeons have privately expressed concern at the idea of taking organs when the deceased person's family is opposed.

Morgan added: 'In cases where someone has not opted out or in, I think the relatives ought to have some say. I think that's where most of the transplantation surgeons are.

'Whatever the legislation says, transplant surgeons said we would not remove those organs if the families were vociferously against because we have a duty of care to those relatives as well as to the patient.'

The Archbishop said he expected the bill to be passed and he would be encouraging people to opt in. He said he thought many Welsh people were unsure what was on the table. 'I don't think that most people realise what the Government is doing. There has been so much confusion with different minsters saying different things at different times.'

The plan is to bring the law into effect in 2015 after an information campaign and discussions with medical practitioners.

Emma Harrison, whose five-year-old son Oliver is waiting for a heart transplant, backed the plans. 'There are not enough hearts, which is incredibly scary. I'm just waiting for the call to say there is a heart for my Ollie. Most people would accept an organ if we needed it. Hopefully we should all be willing to give one too,' she said.

'My Ollie is an amazing, lovely funny guy, he knows he has a poorly heart. We just want him to be able to run up the stairs like his little brother, play football, have a chance of a good life.'

*30 June 2013*

⇨ The above information is reprinted with kind permission from *The Guardian*. Please visit www.theguardian.com for further information.

# Key facts

- In 1969, psychiatrist Elisabeth Kübler-Ross introduced what became known as the 'five stages of grief'. These stages of grief were based on her studies of the feelings of patients facing terminal illness, but many people have generalised them to other types of negative life changes and losses, such as the death of a loved one or a break-up. (page 1)

- US states Massachusetts, Wisconsin and Colorado have banned the use of roadside memorials, while California requires residents to pay a state fee of $1,000. (page 17)

- Every year around half a million people die in England. The success of medicine over the past decades has led to a sustained rise in the average human life expectancy: a third of children born today will live to be 100 years old. (page 18)

- Heart disease was the biggest cause of death in 2012, killing over 64,000 people, followed by dementia and Alzheimer's disease, which caused more than 43,000 deaths, and cerebrovascular diseases which were responsible for more than 35,000 deaths. (page 20)

- Around one in 1,000 deaths in 2012 were among children age one to four years old. The leading cause of death at this age was congenital malformations, deformations and chromosomal abnormalities (14% of boys, 16% of girls). These conditions are usually present at birth or develop shortly after, and include congenital heart defects. (page 20)

- Suicide and injury/poisoning of undetermined intent were the leading cause of death for 20–34-year-olds, for 26% of men and 13% of women. Factors that could lead to these deaths include: traumatic experiences, lifestyle choices such as drug or alcohol misuse, job insecurity and relationship problems. (page 20)

- For people aged 50 and over, the leading causes of death for both men and women are long-term diseases and conditions. Cancer of the trachea, bronchus and lung is the number one cause for women aged 50–64, accounting for 12% of deaths in this group. Breast cancer is the second leading cause of death for 50–64-year-old women, accounting for 11% of deaths in this age group. (page 20)

- 11 babies are stillborn every day in the UK. (page 21)

- Stillbirth is around 15 times more common than cot death. (page 21)

- 83% of people agree that people in Britain are uncomfortable discussing dying and death. 10% disagree. (page 24)

- Fewer than half (41%) of all adults say that they currently have a will. However, that number does rise significantly after the age of 55; almost three quarters of that group do have one (71%). Only two in five (42%) of 45- to 54-year-olds have a will. (page 30)

- The will-writing market in Britain has an estimated value of between £700 million and £900 million. Figures from the probate service show that almost 250,000 families go through probate court every year. 63% of those with a will say they used a law firm of solicitors, compared with 12% who completed the will entirely themselves. (page 30)

- Inheritance tax is due when the value of a person's estate reaches £325,000 or more. Consumer knowledge regarding the specifics of this tax is patchy at best. 28% know exactly what the threshold is, while a quarter (25%) have no idea, and 315 say the threshold is at too low a level. 20% know the rate of tax is 40% but 41% do not know. (page 30)

- Two thirds (66%) of UK adults have had some thoughts about the kind of funeral ceremony they would like. This rises to nearly three quarters (73%) for those aged 55+. An even larger percentage have thought about whether they would like to be buried or cremated, with 91% of the same age group having given this dilemma some consideration. (page 33)

- Almost all (96%) those who organised a funeral in the past five years used a funeral director. (page 33)

- According to the University of Bath's Institute for Policy Research, the average cost of funeral and burial or cremation is now around £3,500. This is a 7.1% rise since last year, and a massive 80% rise since 2004. (page 34)

- Memorial stones are one of the most expensive components of a funeral, costing anything from £200 to several thousand pounds. On average, say Mintel, people pay £864. (page 34)

- Most coffins range in price from between £300 and £1,000. Websites such as comparethecoffin.com can help cut costs and have more information on the many types of coffin available, from traditional wood and metal to cardboard or fabric. (page 34)

- 80% of those tasked with arranging a funeral buy flowers, and spend an average of £160. (page 34)

- 14% of people have shared important online/social media passwords with a friend or family member in case they die. 71% have never thought about what will happen to their digital legacy after they die. (page 38)

## Bereavement

To experience a loss; the loss of a loved one through their death.

## Cemetery/graveyard

Area of land where bodies are buried (unless cremated) and headstones erected to remember the dead. It is usually found attached to a place of worship or crematorium.

## Cremation

A method of disposing of a dead body by burning. The ashes produced are given to the family of the deceased, who can either keep them or choose to scatter them, often in a favourite place of the deceased.

## Coroner

A doctor or lawyer responsible for investigating deaths.

## Death Cafe

A fairly recent idea, a Death Cafe where a group can discuss death, drink tea and eat cake. It is generally a group-directed discussion of death with no agenda, objectives or themes. It is a discussion group rather than a grief support or counselling session, although people grieving may find them helpful.

## Digital legacy

It is not clear on what should happen to a person's online data when they die. This includes all their online accounts, such as e-mail, banking and social networking sites. This can also have an effect on their digital assets, such as music, films and even computer game character – who has the right to decide what will be done with them? Should family members be allowed to have access to them?

## Eco/green funeral

People are now environmentally aware and are now opting for 'eco' funerals. This means that people are planning 'green' funerals that will have a minimal impact on the environment, such as a woodland funeral on an eco site. This can involve a coffin that is biodegradable (e.g. cardboard or willow), no embalming or toxic chemicals are to be used on the body or the coffin and often a tree is planted in place of a headstone.

## Eulogy

A speech delivered at a funeral, praising the person who has died and reminiscing about their life.

## Executor

Someone responsible for the administration of a person's estate after their death, usually nominated by the deceased in their will.

## Funeral

A ceremony, often faith-based and held in a place of worship, which friends and family of the deceased can attend as a way of saying goodbye to their loved one.

## Funeral poverty

Funerals can be expensive: according to the University of Bath's Institute for Policy Research, the average cost of funeral and burial or cremation is now around £3,500. With the growing costs of dying, people simply cannot afford to pay for a funeral – they quite literally 'cannot afford to die'.

## Grief

An intense feeling of sorrow felt after a bereavement; the process of facing the loss of someone you love.

## Headstone

Also known as a tombstone or gravestone. A stone monument erected to a dead person, usually inscribed with their name and dates of birth and death, which friends and family can visit as a way of remembering the dead person. It is usually found in a cemetery.

## Kübler-Ross model (The five stages of grief)

More commonly known as 'the five stages of grief', the Kübler-Ross model suggests that a person who is grieving goes through several emotional responses over time as a reaction to that event: denial, anger, bargaining, depression and acceptance. However, grief is not a linear progression and any one of these five common experiences can occur in any order. Remember, there is no 'right' or 'wrong' way to grieve.

## Living funeral

An end of life celebration arranged while the person, who is most probably suffering from a terminal illness or has a sense that their time is short, is still alive.

## Mourning/grieving

A period during which an individual is in a state of grief. The phrase 'to be in mourning' is more specific – it suggests the observation of certain conventions, for example wearing black.

## Obituary

Notice of a death, usually in a newspaper.

## Organ/tissue donation

The process of a person choosing to donate their organs/tissues for transplant. The NHS Organ Donor Register is a national database that holds the details of people who want to donate their organs when they die - this is an 'opt in' system, so people have to register and sign up for it. One donor can help several people because one person can donate a number of organs: kidneys, liver, heart, lungs, small bowel, pancreas, cornea (eye), bone, skin, heart valves, tendons and cartilage.

## Post-mortem

A medical procedure carried out on a dead body to discover the cause of death where this is unclear.

## Undertaker

Also known as the funeral director. A person who is responsible for organising funerals and preparing bodies for burial or cremation.

## Widow/Widower

A widow is a woman whose husband has died. A man whose wife has died is called a widower.

## Will

A legal document made by a person before their death, containing instructions about matters such as funeral arrangements and division of property in the event of their death.

# Assignments

## Brainstorming

⇨ In small groups, discuss what you know about death and bereavement. Consider the following points:

- What is palliative care?

- What is meant by 'funeral poverty'?

- What is bereavement?

- Why is death often a 'taboo' subject?

## Research

⇨ Find out about the Latin American holiday, Day of the Dead. What are the origins and beliefs surrounding the celebration? Do you think a holiday like this is a good way of remembering those who have died? Write some notes on your findings.

⇨ Find out more about eco-funerals and green burials. Are these a good idea? Would you want the death of someone close to you to be marked in this way? Why, or why not? Write some bullet-point notes and feedback to your class.

⇨ Visit your local cemetery and make rubbings of some of the gravestones which interest you using paper and the side of a crayon. How have people chosen to remember loved ones who have passed away? Do you think the memorials are valuable in preserving the memory of those who have died and helping bereaved people cope with their grief? Discuss your findings with your class.

## Design

⇨ Design a leaflet to give to someone who is grieving. What organisations can they contact for support?

⇨ Choose a religion and research their beliefs and customs surrounding death. What do they believe happens after death? Do they have any burial traditions or ceremonies? Design a brochure that explains your findings, try to include some images or drawings to illustrate your text.

⇨ Design a website for children aged around 11-years-old that will explain death and bereavement. Think of a name for your site, design a logo and plan what kind of information would be on each page.

⇨ Choose an article from this book and create a cartoon to illustrate its themes or ideas.

⇨ Design a poster that will encourage people to talk more openly about death.

## Oral

⇨ 'Death is a part of life. The taboo surrounding the discussion of death and bereavement in our society is deeply unhealthy.' Do you agree? Discuss this viewpoint with a partner.

⇨ Should the organ donation scheme be opt-in or opt-out? Discuss as a class, with half supporting opt-in and the other half arguing for opt-out.

⇨ In pairs, role play a situation in which a parent is explaining the death of a family pet to their 5-year-old child. Consider carefully what you might say to the child to explain the concept of death, and how you might encourage them to deal with their feelings. Take it in turns to play the role of the parent.

⇨ Create a presentation that will explain what someone might need to consider when thinking about their funeral. How much might it cost? Who is responsible for planning, etc.?

## Reading/writing

⇨ Write a list of the different types of memorials that people create in memory of loved ones. How do these memorials offer comfort to those who are left behind?

⇨ Write down as many euphemisms for dying as you can: for example, 'kicking the bucket', 'passing away' and so on. Why do you think we go to such lengths to avoid referring to death directly? Is it right that we should do so? Write a short paragraph explaining your thoughts.

⇨ Read *The Time Keeper* by Mitch Albom. Write a 2-page report that explores how the author explores the concept of death through the two main characters.

⇨ Write a blog entry that explores your feelings on the idea of death cafes. Do you think they are a good idea?

⇨ Watch the 1999 film *Bicentennial Man* and write a review that considers how the film explores the theme of death.

⇨ Try to define 'death'. Write a one sentence explanation and share with your class.

⇨ Read *Why prolonged grief should be listed as a mental disorder* (page 6) and summarise the author's key arguments in bullet-point form.

⇨ Read *What are the top causes of death by age and gender?* (page 20) and write a summary for your school newspaper.

⇨ Read the article *Your digital legacy – what happens to your online data after you die?* (page 37). What have you learned from this article? Write no more than 200 words.

# Acknowledgements

The publisher is grateful for permission to reproduce the material in this book. While every care has been taken to trace and acknowledge copyright, the publisher tenders its apology for any accidental infringement or where copyright has proved untraceable. The publisher would be pleased to come to a suitable arrangement in any such case with the rightful owner.

Images

Cover and pages ii, 11, 10, 16 and 17: iStock; page 10 © Jackie Staines.

Illustrations

Don Hatcher: pages 5 & 18. Simon Kneebone: pages 8 & 32. Angelo Madrid: pages 29 & 37.

Additional acknowledgements

Editorial on behalf of Independence Educational Publishers by Cara Acred.

With thanks to the Independence team: Mary Chapman, Sandra Dennis, Christina Hughes, Jackie Staines and Jan Sunderland.

Cara Acred

Cambridge

September 2014